Principles and Practices of Professional Consulting

Steven C. Stryker

GOVERNMENT INSTITUTES
A division of
THE SCARECROW PRESS, INC.
Lanham • Toronto • Plymouth, UK
2011

 **Government
Institutes**

Published by Government Institutes
An imprint of The Scarecrow Press, Inc.
A wholly owned subsidiary of The Rowman & Littlefield Publishing Group, Inc.
4501 Forbes Boulevard, Suite 200, Lanham, Maryland 20706
http://www.govinstpress.com

Estover Road, Plymouth PL6 7PY, United Kingdom

British Library Cataloguing in Publication Information Available

Library of Congress Cataloging-in-Publication Data
Stryker, Steven C.
  Principles and practices of professional consulting / Steven C. Stryker.
  p.   cm.
  Includes bibliographical references and index.
  ISBN 978-1-60590-721-5 (cloth : alk. paper) — ISBN 978-1-60590-722-2
(electronic)
  1. Consultants. I. Title.
  HD69.C6S87 2011
  001—dc22

                                                           2010037476

∞^TM The paper used in this publication meets the minimum requirements
of American National Standard for Information Sciences—Permanence of
Paper for Printed Library Materials, ANSI/NISO Z39.48-1992.

Printed in the United States of America

*For Hubert Bermont, who had the faith and confidence in my ability to
ask not just why, but why not?
Thanks for the support which has engendered my career.*

Contents

Preface

Consulting is a profession that has traditionally been taught experientially—in the "learning by doing" school of thought. Few attempts have been made to establish, as a distinct body of knowledge, the tenets and techniques of consulting. Although consultants the world over influence the outcome of major endeavors in management, finance, government, engineering, and countless other fields of specialization, seldom has consulting been treated as a serious business, with a past, present, and future.

I recognize that consulting is more than a profession, a vocation, or a discipline, although it is all of those. This book presents consulting as a dynamic process, the current conduct of which rests on a discernable set of principles and practices which in turn have emerged from a study of the history of consulting as a separate field of learning. It thoroughly examines the major facets of a consulting assignment, methodically coupled with the practical skills and techniques that are the tools of the successful consultant. Case examples, based on real-life situations, aptly demonstrate the applicability of the material to current consulting activities.

Consulting is thus not just a job, a position, or a discipline. Consulting is a lifestyle of providing abilities and means of assisting clients to achieve the movement from old to new. It defines an interaction mode which transmits insight and procedure that clients can keep using long after the assignment is over. Gratification in consulting is derived from understanding the motivations, limitations, and possibilities for yourself and your work.

This book is intended for an audience of interested professionals of various disciplines, whether self-employed or part of a large or small organization, as well as for students. It dispels the notion that consulting is far more art than science; art consists chiefly of arcane bits of knowledge and craft that can only be mastered by a few individuals with the right combination of esoteric wisdom and specialized experience. This book describes, through a comprehensive approach that unites theory and practice, consulting principles that can be grasped by anyone wishing to expand his ability to initiate and implement organizational change. It lays the groundwork for the perceptive handling of each assignment through the integration of knowledge, experience, and instinct.

Acknowledgments

My thanks go to the many people who have given time and effort to move this book toward publication. The Library of Congress was particularly helpful and generous in allowing me to read all there is to read on the subject. Appreciation goes to Mr. Wright and Mr. Martin of the Research Facilities Office, Mrs. Blair of the Loan Division, and Gary Jensen, Sandy Long, and Samuel M. Andrusko of the Thomas Jefferson Reading Room. Others who provided resources include Hillel Weinberg of Congressman Gelman's Office, Joan Stewart of the William Morris Agency, and Jerry Schwinn of Hagler, Bailly & Co. Special thanks go to Kathleen Regiec for editing the manuscript, Mia Smith for faithfully typing it, Amy Arutt and Jeff Rich for reading it, and Myer Feldman for providing photocopying support. In addition, the encouragement of my extended family, with particular thanks to my mother, motivated me to unflinchingly pursue this project.

Chapter 1

Introduction

OVERVIEW

Beginning a new activity can be an anxiety-ridden venture into the unknown.

Common questions asked are, What am I getting myself into? Will it be interesting? Can I find the "truth" that I'm seeking, and will it be meaningful? What will happen if I fail? All these questions imply a curiosity, but also a tension about the endeavor to be undertaken. The challenge is to keep the creative energy high by staying motivated.

This book examines the consulting process in a framework that allows each reader to find his own meaning. The basic principles of consulting are built upon through examples and extended by discussion about areas related to consulting. The concepts and information presented are neither "sacred" nor a fixed set of immutable laws, but rather a flow of ideas that are subject to interpretation which can lead to subsequent modification of behavior.

The format of the book is more or less uniform. Each chapter is divided into five parts.

An introductory paragraph or two stages the chapter. This is followed, where relevant, by a skills section which enhances the use of the chapter ideas. The next section, the body, concisely presents the central concepts of the chapter. These ideas are refined by pertinent case examples and/or special, related topics. At the end of each chapter is a synopsis and extension of the principles. This final section uses past chapters to build a wider viewpoint so the reader can better understand the chapter material. The chapter summary serves as a prelude to the succeeding chapter. Books and articles are cited throughout each chapter. Where multiple sources are cited together, they are listed in the order of their importance. All material not referenced is my own.

COMMUNICATION FRAMEWORK

When thinking of consulting, certain images usually come to mind: help, assistance, performance, business, expert, advice, outsider, giver, teacher, idea seller, fixer, scapegoat, exploiter, behind-the-scenes influencer, and other related terms. Basically, each time we learn something, we are involved in a consulting activity. Often in the past, learning occurred as a direct response to extreme changes in external conditions, usually crisis. One of the distinguishing features of the current era is our potential to learn to be more effective in responding to change per se. This means learning how to *plan for change*. The goal of this book is to explain how consulting can be a prime motivating force for effective change.

To discuss coherently the subject of consulting, both reader and writer must agree on certain words and concepts. A common language allows the learner to agree or disagree, to probe some points more deeply than others, and to develop an overall sense of the material.

In addition, the concept of consulting can be explained independently of its required skills or assignment areas. The elements of the consulting activity can be described as follows:

- The *context* of consulting is the *organization*. This is a group of people whose purpose is to engage in a societal activity that provides goods or services. Examples of organizations include a private company, institution, association or public agency, or some part of these entities. There is a contact person in each organization who generally makes fundamental decisions about the organization's activities. The contact person senses the need for consulting and decides to employ the services of the consultant. The contact person is called the *client*. The members of the organization who will work with the client and the consultant are called the *client group*.
- The *content* of consulting is the *issue*. This is simply a technical or personnel problem within the organization. The cause of the problem can be found in old situations or new developments within the organization. The issue could be a technical or personnel problem (most issues have a little of both). The successful completion of a consulting assignment will result in a *resolution* of one or both of these problems (Kubr 1976).

- The *catalyst* of consulting is the *process*. This is a sequence of flexible steps that are tailored to the particular organizational situation to resolve the issue.
- The *collaborator* of consulting is the *consultant*. This person has a disciplinary education with experiential training in the consulting process. He is not directly involved in or affected by the issue. The consultant may be in another part of the client's organization, may represent an outside organization or group of colleagues, or may act independently. It is the consultant's responsibility to carry out the consulting process in an efficient and effective way and to produce results that will satisfy the client. There is usually some form of a *contract*, either a formal one or a letter of agreement, specifying the terms of the consulting assignment.

The preceding definition of a consultant could apply to a lawyer, financial counselor, teacher, engineer, accountant, and so on. Yet these professionals work for or with the client on an ongoing basis, completing tasks in a disciplinary area (law, construction, auditing, etc.) and providing information needed to operate the organization (Seney 1963). In general, a consultant seeks to resolve issues of a one-shot, interdisciplinary nature through a continuous, short-term arrangement. The consultant assists with the client's response to changes in the structure and/or function of the organization.

So, the definition of *consulting* is an *assignment* in which a *consultant* and a *client* seek to *resolve* a *client organizational issue* using a specified *process*. There are certainly variations of this definition, such as consultants consulting with other consultants or consulting with intermediaries about the client (e.g., teachers with parents about their students, doctors with other doctors about their patients). Consultants may also act as arbitrators, adversaries, or coordinators within an organization or among organizations.

Yet, the goal in these modified forms of consulting is the same as that of regular consulting: to provide responsive and accurate aid for resolving a particular issue.

The outcome of the consulting engagement is *resolution of the issue*. Resolution means *change*. In this context, change means differences produced by the consultation in the perceptions and motivations of the client and client group, and in the structure and operations of the organization. The changes are generally measured, evaluated, and reported by the consultant. These changes also have ramifications for the consultant, the consulting firm, and future contact with the client, which will be discussed later in greater detail. Today there are increasing pressures to bring about change and increasing frustrations in trying to do so. The consultant must assess how much change the client is capable of making. Realizing the need for changes and making them will be treated here as two separate but interconnected functions.

The primary function of the consultant is to prepare the client for change. The consultant must make change acceptable without sacrificing the objectives of the client, the client group, and the organization.

Chapter 2

The History of Consulting

OVERVIEW

History is not often included in discussions about the consulting field. The implied reasons are that consulting is a relatively new area of human endeavor having little history; that tracing the roots of consulting will give little insight into its practice; and that seeing the evolution of this vocation will not be helpful in deciding how to change its practice.

This chapter will show how these are false assumptions. Following a special topic section, the introduction sets forth the historical roots of consulting and describes the subsequent presentation. Next, the two threads of consulting history are separately elucidated, and then the various kinds of consulting activities are noted. The theme stressed in this chapter and reiterated in the concluding chapter is the same: namely, consulting as it is practiced today is the intertwining of its historical influences.

SPECIAL TOPIC: THE RUDIMENTS OF CONSULTING

The time-honored practice of seeking advice from experts, elders, or wise politicians is well established in history. An example of how a leader benefited from the suggestions of an elder is found in the story of Moses. He had sent his wife and children to stay with his father-in-law, Jethro, while he led the Jews out of Egypt. When Jethro heard that the Exodus had taken place, he brought the family to join Moses at the wilderness encampment at Sinai.

On the first morning of his short visit, Jethro watched Moses settling disputes. All those in the camp with disputes would stand before the seated judge. They would wait hours to see Moses, since he considered many cases. When Jethro inquired as to why Moses adjudicated alone, Moses replied that the people expected him solely to interpret the law for them.

Jethro agreed that a legal and moral advisor was necessary, but thought the task too great for any one person. Each case would not receive the attention it merited. Jethro suggested that Moses choose "able men such as fear God, men of truth, hating unjust gain; and place such over them to be rulers of thousands, rulers of hundreds, rulers of fifty and rulers of ten." Moses should teach these people the statutes and the laws and should "show them the way they must walk, and the work that they must do." Every great dispute would be brought directly to Moses, but every small dispute would be judged by those appointed as arbitrators.

In this way, Jethro said, the cases would be settled, with each person able to obtain quick justice in his own part of the camp. Having seen this system of justice instituted, Jethro departed for his home in Midian.

HISTORY OF CONSULTING: AN INTRODUCTION

As shown by the biblical vignette, the ability to recognize and diagnose issues in an environment of authority and influence goes back to the beginning of Western civilization.

However, our discussion focuses on the period during which consulting has been continuously practiced, from about 1870. All forms of consulting described here refer exclusively to its practice within an organizational structure. The development of psychiatric consulting, for example, would be relevant only as it relates to the purpose of the organization. The discussion is limited to those theories and incidents which helped stimulate a wider acceptance, use, or development of consulting services.

To set the stage for this historical presentation, the origin of the consulting process must first be understood. The process of consulting is derived from Roger Bacon's formulation of a method for performing scientific research in the 13th century (Wells 1931). As used today, the scientific method has seven steps.

1. Observation
2. Examination
3. Hypothesis
4. Experiment

5. Results
6. Conclusions
7. Extensions and modifications

Thus, each kind of consulting is derived as a process of inquiry from the scientific method.

There are two general historic strains of consulting: scientific management and behavioral management. Each strain has three development phases—an early, middle, and modern phase. This characterization of consulting implies a historical perspective with a singular origin, divergent in consulting procedures, yet following a similar development cycle.

Strain 1: Development of Scientific Management

The concept of consulting derives from the scientific method. The environment of consulting developed during the Industrial Revolution, the period of history that saw the 18th-century world of the agrarian worker transformed into a 19th-century assembly-line, factory environment. This transformation meant that the worker gave up property ownership and self-sufficiency for the higher wages of the factories, at the cost of a dependence on industry for his survival. In other words, the labor conditions and personal satisfaction of the employee were subservient to the output of goods. Innovations in working conditions, such as health, safety, or leisure improvements, came about by trial and error. A few entrepreneurs realized that no real gains could be made in the productivity of laborers by such a haphazard process. They sought, instead, more consistent and comprehensive means of improving the production environment. However, these "reforms" were few, far between, and short lived (George 1968; Klein 1977).

Nevertheless, from the sporadic application of insight by factory owners to the worker situation came the seeds of a new concept—that of factory management. But, for those first factory controllers of the workforce, efficiency was the goal. Efficiency meant more output per worker per day. Achieving this goal required more than seat-of-the-pants understanding. Into this milieu came Frederick Taylor, an engineer whose research work spanned 50 years—1880 to 1930. His contributions have had an unbroken influence on the development of management science. From Taylor's observations, his examinations of the work experience in factories, and his subsequent writing, we find the following picture of management-labor relations in the last quarter of the 19th century.

Managers knew of only two ways to get more product out of workers: a little persuasion and a lot of coercion. The average worker found ample room for resenting this kind of treatment—resentment to match the already oppressive working environment. Were managers of factories so completely callous as not to see the blindness of their ways? Several reasons were given for this state of affairs. Managers just did not understand their responsibilities toward worker "advancement." Therefore, decisions of factory overseers and owners with respect to workers were based only on intuition or past experience. There were no standards that had been developed and applied to the tasks of the laborer. Most workers were doing jobs for which they had almost no ability or aptitude. At this early stage in factory management, the owners gave little thought to the likelihood of high productivity providing incentives for both managers and workers (George 1968).

Given these hypotheses, Taylor set out to discover more about the workplace. One of the major contributions he made to the emerging understanding of labor activities was the time-motion study of workers' tasks. At the Midvale Steel Plant in Pennsylvania, Taylor dissected each job function to find its basic elements, timed those elements, and sought to modify them to increase the efficiency of each job function and thus the output of each worker. From this and other studies, he developed a coordinated system of shop management that he called "scientific management." To correct the management-labor quandary, Taylor (1947) suggested the following:

1. The use of research methods rather than rules of thumb to handle manager and worker relations
2. The introduction and incorporation of work standards in every domain of management to increase and sustain higher rates of worker output
3. The development of job placement methods to further these standards
4. The payment of high wages and the achievement of low unit production costs as two indicators of competent management
5. The use of cooperation and mutual understanding as the only effective means to satisfy the basic desires and needs of management and labor

Taylor's era saw the rise of management as a separate field of learning. He, like other major contributors mentioned later, realized that a science of management needed a comprehensive approach incorporating the planning, organizing, directing, and controlling functions of a firm. In his early days, Taylor was widely heralded as an innovator, a purveyor of ideas founded in experience with immediate and measurable application. The original thrust of Taylor's principles helped make existing management practices more precise without changing the fundamental philosophy or role of the manager. Taylor subscribed to one philosophy throughout his professional career. Its tenets were that human and machine resources are not mutually adaptable, but that the worker functions instead as an appendage to the industrial machine (Etzioni 1964). Second, according to Taylor, "a knowledgeable manager should give a worker only one thing—that which he wanted the most—the chance to make as much money as possible" (Klein 1977, 24). Third, increased productivity among the workforce would prevent layoffs (Koehler 1976). Fourth, unions would not be necessary when the scientific management approach was utilized (Klein 1977).

There were clearly influences and challenges to Taylor's contributions. Two of his contemporaries, Frank and Lillian Gilbreth, furthered the accuracy of time-motion studies in the first decade of the 20th century. However, they differed with Taylor by saying that unions were needed and that money was not the only motivation to spur increased productivity. Henry L. Gantt, a colleague of Taylor, developed a task and bonus system, an extension of Taylor's output-incentive system. For production control, Gantt introduced a chart which portrayed the amount of time needed to perform various activities.

Managers could then compare actual versus planned performance on this Gantt chart. In 1912, along with Taylor and the Gilbreths, Harrington Emerson, a consulting engineer, developed a set of efficiency principles for use in management operations. The principles called for standards, planning, control, and rewards, as well as defined goals and objectives, discipline, and *competent counsel*. His rationale for competent counseling was that no single executive could master all functions in an organization (Emerson 1913). Emerson affirmed the need for outside expertise, which encouraged the small number of fledgling consulting firms to set fees based on a professional scale. Thus, in this early period of scientific management, principles and techniques were developed to make commonsense approaches to management more rational.

The middle period, from 1920 to 1940, had a different emphasis. During the 1920s and 1930s, the established consulting firms grew and prospered. Consulting remained primarily a luxury of large corporations, 19th-century elite. The consulting enterprise consisted of a handful of prestigious firms in major cities and skilled individual practitioners calling themselves "industrial engineers," whose specialties were assembly-line and other production techniques, personnel and industrial relations, and adaptation of technologies. Yet, these consulting firms and individuals failed to seek a broader spectrum of work among existing clients or to attract smaller organizations to the profitable use of consulting services (Klein 1977). The time and motion studies continued, and in 1939, a training school opened at Lake Placid, New York, to teach the theory and practice of work simplification. It was run by Allan H. Mogensen (Raybould and Minter 1971).

The efforts at extending general theories of management took an interesting turn with the work of Chester I. Barnard, a telephone company executive. In his view, the organization existed to fulfill certain biological, physical, and social wants of the individual through its consciously coordinated activities (Barnard 1938). The executive was present to provide the communication, recruitment, and goal definition functions of the organization. Yet, workers complied with the results of the executive's efforts only when they understood and believed them to be consistent with the purpose of the organization as well as their own beliefs and values (George 1968). Barnard's philosophy involved a fundamental switch in emphasis, from the view that what is good for the organization is good for the individual to the view that what is good for the consortium of individuals is now good for the organization. To take this perception a step further, the continuance of an organization, according to Barnard, depended upon the delicate balance between the individual member's contributions and the satisfaction he derived. Implicit in Barnard's philosophy was the Taylor notion that cooperation of the individual would only occur through material and monetary inducements.

The modern period, since 1940, has seen the rise of new management techniques, the proliferation of consulting firms serving all sectors of the economy in domestic and foreign assignments, and the practice of using an integrated management approach to dealing with issues. The war effort of the early 1940s spawned new techniques of handling goods shipments, planning and executing production schedules, allocating scarce resources, carrying out logistic maneuvers, and formulating policy. To successfully handle these complex tasks in a short time, the scientific method and its practice by Taylor were extended into a new area called *Operations Research* (OR). In an OR assignment, people with various backgrounds are brought together as an interdisciplinary team to find solutions to issues. The approach consists of

- Formulating an issue or problem,
- Constructing a mathematical model of the system,
- Deriving a solution from the model,
- Testing the model and its solutions for internal consistency,
- Establishing controls over the solution(s) in order to incorporate external changes within the model, and
- Implementing the solution.

This approach provided managers with a quantitative basis for making decisions. Its application to the management situation helped foster much consulting work for a broad spectrum of private clients.

One effect of OR was to extend the time-motion studies of an earlier era. A new tool, *methods analysis*, was added to measure how well production procedures were functioning and to point out ways of increasing output. These techniques continue to be researched and applied today. In fact, corporate interest in these industrial engineering techniques has kept a large number of specialized consultants or consulting firms well reimbursed for services rendered.

OR also had the effect of creating a civilian public sector demand for consulting services. Imaginative consulting firms began applying OR techniques to the wide array of public issue concerns. This spawned new techniques and new applications. As a consequence, consulting quickly grew to meet the megadollar demand for its services. And yet, the issues that public sector consultants have focused on reflect the "bandwagon" perspective of their clients. In the early 1960s much consulting was done in transportation planning. In the late 1960s and early 1970s efforts were directed at environmental matters. The 1980s and 1990s saw the consulting focus shift and deepen using information technology to address a myriad of new applications. Concurrent with this development, consulting work became more defined in terms of projects—specific engagements with a defined beginning, middle, and end. And, in the last decade, the gamut of public needs have flourished as government consulting activity. (Future directions of public sector consulting are explored in the last chapter.)

The private sector had also not waned in its use of consultants. Many were retained to implement the complete guide to management, including planning, organizing, directing, and controlling. The person responsible for setting forth the theory of generalized management was Henri Fayol (1949). He formulated a universal theory of management independent of the form of the organization. According to Fayol, the organization should be governed by a centralized authority and all management tasks should be based on a set of explicit, objective criteria. Performance should be directly related to the goals of the organization in order to achieve the highest production level possible within cost constraints. Fayol initiated the concepts of long-range planning and forecasting that were used by many firms with consultants' assistance. In addition, project management techniques, government contracts, and generalized management frameworks all combined to boost institutional use of consultants in education, criminal apprehension, hospital cost containment, recreational land use, and other areas.

During the modern period, consultants from developed countries influenced the rate of technical and social progress in developing countries.

Spurred by the United Nations, the World Bank, the Agency for International Development, and others, contacts were established in almost every urban locale in the African, Asian, Caribbean, and South American land masses. The major clients tended to be the governments, and the major type of project tended to be engineering based. The basic obstacles faced by most outside consultants were the definition and effective use of their role (Francis 1976). In the last decade, some overseas assignments have had consultants organizing for and adapting to change.

Thus, the scientific management influence on consulting can be viewed much as one would perceive the evolution of modern technology: from a few perceptive and influential minds came the theory of consulting and various approaches to it. This has resulted in a plethora of private consulting firms forming to provide service for large companies. The industrial mobilization of the 1940s caused both new techniques and a new client, the government, to be included in the array of consulting activities. From the influence of these events, new consulting firms were formed to serve various types of governmental entities.

Profit and not-for-profit consulting firms, institutes, and internal consulting groups provided a broad spectrum of technical and managerial support services. To succinctly typify the client's growing need for consulting services, consider that the bookkeeper of the 1920s who had never heard of consulting became the accountant of the 1940s (working with auditors periodically), who, in turn, became the financial manager of the 1960s and 1970s, who became the financial officer from the 1980s onward who frequently sought accounting consultation.

Strain 2: Development of Behavioral Management

Parallel to the evolution of scientific management, the early phase of behavioral management began with a seminal thinker who articulated one of the cornerstones of behavioral management. Henry Gantt was one of the first advocates of employee training. He felt this training should be a direct management responsibility. However, Gantt was still heavily influenced by the scientific management perspective. One of the founders of industrial psychology, Hugo Munsterberg, professor of experimental psychology at Harvard, used quantitative tools to measure psychological differences between individual employees in their workplace (George 1968).

The middle period (1920–1940) was characterized by recognition of the need for a personnel department within the organizational framework. Elton Mayo, a Harvard professor, was concerned with the major elements of employee motivation. He conducted a five-year experiment at the Hawthorne Works of the Western Electric Company to try to discover those elements (Mayo 1933). In 1932, his results showed that nonmaterial incentives, such as attention, freedom to set one's work pace, and communication between workers and researchers, could have an impact equal to or greater than material incentives in motivating employees. Mayo also discovered that the working group to which an individual belongs can exercise an informal authority over this person which can subordinate his will to the will of the group, sometimes to the person's detriment, and exert more influence over the individual than the formal authority of management.

Mayo concluded that management needed to foster a new way of relating to employees that reflected an increased emphasis on the individual's willingness to cooperate with the managerial staff. This scheme required a coordinated organizational and communications network. Mayo's findings called into question one of Taylor's basic tenets—that monetary incentives are the only cause of high productivity. Mayo's suggestions also laid the groundwork for personnel training and counseling techniques, which were more fully developed in the modern period.

Mayo's perceptions were sustained by one of the foremost independent consultants of the 1920s, Mary Parker Follett. From her experience in consulting with industrial and political leaders, she realized that an individual had similar motives and drives whether on the job or not. She concluded that the objective of the manager is to nurture group efforts, not to force and drive individuals (George 1968).

In the modern period (1940–present), we find an approach to handling behavioral issues in an organizational context that grew from the efforts of the early and middle periods. The approach is called *Organization Development* (OD). OD is a type of consulting used to assist managers in improving the quality of employee-oriented organizational activities.

Tools and techniques used in OD came from social behavior study and learning theory research, as well as from scientific management. OD places emphasis on the human factors and data inherent in the organization-employee relationship. OD strategies can be used to help employees become more committed and more adaptable, which ultimately improves the organization as a whole.

The concept and its application were stressed in the late 1940s by Leland Bradford, a training supervisor for the Federal Security Agency. He applied OD to a program of integrated, long-term training, which was initiated to replace the piecemeal training efforts that concentrated only on basic job skills. One of the early techniques of OD—the learning laboratory—came from Bradford's shop (McGill 1977). It provided an opportunity for employees to share personal concerns with their fellow workers and was initially well received. However, when the participants returned to their offices, credibility gaps developed because of the differences in perceptions of job performance among managers, peers, and subordinates. Changes that were agreed upon in the learning laboratory often did not carry over into the workplace. A modified form of laboratory training evolved that attempted to close this interaction gap by integrating individual behavior within the organization. In this way, new management efforts would be subject to consensus and, if found favorable, would be given the support of all those affected. This technique was also applied in a modified learning laboratory program set up in 1954 by the California State Personnel Board. Based on the experience of the board's managers, the program's emphasis was on increasing interpersonal skills.

The Foundation for Research on Human Behavior was founded in the late 1950s in Ann Arbor, Michigan, and helped to speed the acceptance of OD principles in many types of organizations. This institute is prototypical of other places of management and social psychology research. Using the experimental orientations of Munsterberg and Follett, the results from these places have extended our knowledge of the physiological motivations and the psychological effects of change. These experimental results helped establish OD's reputation in assisting organizations with change. It was not until the late 1970s that books providing a comprehensive picture of the techniques and practical strategies of OD began to appear (Margulies 1978; G. Lippett 1978; McGill 1977; French 1978).

Another influence on OD is the extension of Mayo's work in the modern period. Rensis Likert conducted studies of management-employee relations in the latter half of the 1950s. His results showed that employee-centered managers, who perceived their role as one of removing obstacles to effective employee performance, were more successful than job-centered managers, who saw their role as one of obtaining maximum efficiency of operations and output per employee. The latter approach may achieve its purposes, but not without consequent job dissatisfaction and possible job turnover. The key to effective management, Likert (1961) stated, is the degree to which employees are able to participate in the goal setting and decision making of organizations. Likert's philosophy and results were extended to create programs of action-oriented research and planned change, two cornerstones of OD practices today (Margulies 1972; Huse 1975; G. Lippett 1978; "How to Conduct a Post-Mortem" 1965).

Throughout the 1970s and 1980s OD became a more established field with courses and programs being offered in business, education, and administration curricula. In the 1990s and the first decade of the 21st century, OD continued to grow and evolve and its influences could be seen in theories and strategies such as total quality management, team building, job enrichment, and reengineering.

Whereas the scientific approach to management helps organizations attain higher levels of efficiency, the behavioral approach reaches for deeper levels of effectiveness. The primary emphasis of the behaviorists has been on research, experimentation, and implementation of methods and ideas that open an organization to participative management.

From the narrow-skills training days, the organizational efforts have grown to a wide variety of stimuli to assist employee and management learning. OD efforts continue to be directed at improving communication throughout the organization's sphere of influence—particularly with the fast-evolving social media technologies. As at the beginning, OD's value today is in optimizing an organization's needs and goals with the needs, wants, and personal satisfaction of its employees, for "the assumption [is] that industrial peace would be an automatic product of honest communication between management and labor" (Koehler 1976, 30).

Case Example 2.1. Automation via Scientific Management

The First Deposit Bank of a small, southeastern town acquired many new customers as industry moved into the community. The manual, backup methods of keeping track of withdrawals, deposits, new customers, check accounting, and other services were overloaded and in need of attention. Cy Berns of JCN Consultants was called in to handle the situation. He established an immediate professional rapport over a business dinner with Jack Olway, vice president in charge of operations. The situation was defined in these terms by Cy Berns: "The throughput of transactions exceeds the capability of the bank to absorb any additional increase in customer demands. I would therefore suggest an immediate cost-benefit analysis of all alternatives." Jack Olway agreed, then asked, "Does this mean new information technology [IT] will be coming into our operations?"

Berns spent the next month carefully costing out equipment, drawing up a schedule of changes needed to complete the automation, developing a timeline for implementing the changes, putting together a package of various technology options, drawing up flowcharts of the new automation equipment, and creating a presentation for Olway's approval. A week later, Berns gave his marketing pitch to Olway, complete with recommendations as to which automation option to buy. Olway presented these findings to the Board of Governors; they were approved. Olway said during the meeting, "If anyone can improve things around here, it is JCN."

Three months later the IT solution was in full swing. Cy Berns worked closely with Jack Olway and his people, guiding them step-by-step on the installation and integration of the equipment and providing people from JCN to give instruction and updates (in addition to the automation firm's representatives). The IT solution was completed in only six weeks. Yet, the JCN representatives remained at the bank for close to three months afterward. An advertising campaign by the bank produced a 30% increase in customer service demand over the next quarter. The enhanced automated operations were able to handle the increase, but manual backup continued for another nine months.

Case Example 2.2. Automation via Behavioral Management

At the fourth bank board meeting after the automation was complete, Jack Olway said that his personnel turnover had increased since the computer system began functioning. He asked for the Board of Governors' sanction to look into this disturbing turn of events. With board permission, Olway called an industrial psychologist he knew who recommended he contact Organization Resources and Education (ORE). A representative from ORE, Patti Insitte, came to see Olway the following week. After explaining the situation to Insitte, Olway asked what her firm could do. "There are no pat answers or easy solutions," Insitte remarked, "but it sounds like some valuable information has not been transmitted to those who work with the machines day by day."

Further discussion ensued and it was decided that Insitte would conduct a two-day seminar entitled "Better Ways of Working with Information Technology." Olway informed his subordinates of the seminar, and on the appointed day, time, and place (near, but not in the office) the seminar began. Insitte started by having people sitting comfortably at a conference table, introducing themselves, and saying a few words about what they do, and how long they had been doing it. She then gave a short presentation on the fears of working with machines. Following a short break, Insitte passed around a questionnaire regarding her presentation for every participant to fill out. Next, she said that those who wished could read their comments aloud. At first, people were very reluctant to share. Finally one person across from Insitte asked, "Will these comments help us at the next salary review?" That broke the ice, and the participants bantered about the fun and frustrations of automation until the lunch break.

In the afternoon, Insitte gave a short slide show on how a computer system can work for each individual. Groups of three or four were formed and given the assignment of preparing a group help plan for adjusting to the upgraded IT environment. This activity took the rest of that afternoon and continued into the evening for some of the groups.

The next morning each group gave a ten-minute talk on its plan. After all the groups had their say, the floor was again open for free-for-all discussion. After lunch, Insitte came back with lists of comments on the difficulties with automation that she had collected both inside and outside of class. She shared them with the participants and they discussed ways to alleviate them. The participants decided that the suggestions would be written up, categorized in order of importance, and presented to the board at its next meeting via Olway, who actively participated in the seminar.

Insitte kept in touch with Olway and learned that the board had given carte blanche to the suggestions. Six months later Patti Insitte saw Jack Olway at a Rotary Club meeting and inquired about progress at the bank. "It is clear," Olway affirmed, "that your time was worth every penny." Employee turnover had dropped to almost zero, and IT operations had improved to the point where manual backup functions could be almost completely eliminated.

CONSULTING ACTIVITIES

There is a wide array of services that consultants provide for clients in all sectors of our society. Trying to pinpoint the exact nature of these services is difficult. A consultant's job is defined as much by what he knows as by how he applies it. Thus, consulting services are a combination of learned skills and organizational requirements. Attempts to classify consulting activities are incomplete and imprecise at best. Those who have tried to put together a list of consulting endeavors, such as Hunt (1977), French (1978), or the Association of Consulting Engineers of Canada (1976), have concentrated on one kind of consulting—business, training, or engineering, respectively. These are only a part of the spectrum of services that consultants provide. Table 2.1 is a chart of various consulting endeavors. The table follows the earlier definition of consulting in an organizational context. (Indeed, for individual consulting needs there is a different array, including such consultants as bridal, estate planning, or catering.) The chart illustrates the scope of consulting work that exists in the private, institutional, and public sectors today.

Traditionally, business, engineering, and management consulting tended to use scientific management principles, while education and social service consulting leaned toward behavioral management principles. Specialized consultants often used both in their assignments. Today, both strains are increasingly found, with varying degrees of emphasis, in all consulting areas.

Table 2.1. Classification of Consulting Activities

Branch of Consulting	Types of Clients	Areas of Consulting	Services Provided
Business	Private firms Institutions	General management	Organizational studies Long-range planning
		Finance	Accounting and budgeting procedures Financial feasibility studies Cash-flow and cost-forecasting analyses Pension fund assessments Merger and acquisition advice
		Personnel	Job administration and evaluation Work measurement and compensation Training and development
		Production	Production methods and control Human factors
		Marketing	Market analyses and sales forecasting Distribution methods Advertising and promotion
		Data processing	Equipment surveys and feasibility studies Automation evaluation and processes Technical analyses and scheduling algorithms
		Transportation/ communication	Resource utilization studies
Engineering	Private firms Institutions Government	Project	Feasibility studies Preliminary designs
		Construction	Scheduling methods Regulatory compliance oversight Cost and labor control
		Maintenance	Equipment and structural schedules and techniques Health and safety evaluations

Management	Government	Policy	Policy analysis and evaluation
			Regulatory analyses and impact studies
			Public participation/information dissemination
		Program	Program coordination and review
			Budgetary planning
			Technology transfer
		Organization	Strategic planning
			Reorganization support
			Interorganizational liaison
Education	Institutions	Curriculum	General development and assessment
	Private firms		Special programs
	Government	Communication	Pair or group dynamics
			Network-building tools
			Classroom processes
		Conflict resolution	Community feedback techniques
Specialized	Private firms	Employment	Recruitment procedures
	Institutions		Management appraisal
	Government	Labor relations	Labor contract negotiator
			Arbitration mediator
		Public relations	Advertising campaigns
			Public opinion assessment
			Conference management
			Presentation services
		Advisory	Expert advice or testimony

REVIEW AND EXTENSION

These pages have been an exploration of the history of consulting. Unlike the history of wars, there are no winners or losers. Unlike the history of civilizations, there are no declines in cultural influence. But, like wars and civilizations, there is a distinct goal—to improve the means by which organizations function. The means are the people, the functions are planning, organizing, directing, and controlling. The contributors to the field have stimulated the improvement of organizations by developing better techniques, concepts, or services, as shown in table 2.2. These activities, in turn, have helped stimulate client interest with a subsequent increase in consulting assignments and firms.

There is great diversity in the various fields and endeavors of consulting, making a precise definition of a consulting assignment difficult.

Table 2.2.   Historical Management Perspectives

	Perspective	
Period	*Scientific Management*	*Behavioral Management*
Early (1890–1920)	Few consulting firms Use of scientific method Emphasis on efficiency Principles of management articulated Time-motion studies Accent on material incentives	No consulting firms Based on scientific method Emphasis on effectiveness Accent on employee education
Middle (1920–1940)	Private sector consulting Extended scientific method Emphasis on efficiency Principles of management extended Work simplification Accent on material and individual incentives	Consulting institutes Based on behavior studies Emphasis on effectiveness Employee-centered management Accent on personnel department
Modern (1940–present)	Public-private sector consulting Based on Operations Research methods and techniques Emphasis on efficiency Generalized management principles Methods analysis Accent on material and individual incentives International consulting	Public-private sector consulting Based on Organization Development methods and techniques Emphasis on effectiveness Participative management Accent on personnel training and counseling

Areas of consulting application tend to change sooner than the principles of consulting practice. Change, as most OD practitioners would agree, is a major element of consulting. George Santayana asserted that those who don't learn from the mistakes of history are doomed to repeat them. Thus, if we view change as an organizational way of life, the following chapters can generate active insights into the effective uses of consulting.

Chapter 3

The Consulting Process

OVERVIEW

If the key to discussing consulting lies in the definition, then the key to practicing it lies in the consulting process. The steps of a consulting assignment will be presented in this chapter, based on the evolution of consulting described in the previous chapter. The assumptions implicit in the process will precede its description; the reasons why consultants are employed by clients will follow the process description. The various roles consultants assume will be examined and related to the process description. From these topics the responsibilities of both consultant and client will emerge. The consulting process is the heart of consulting and is the cornerstone upon which all subsequent chapters are built.

FUNDAMENTALS OF THE CONSULTING PROCESS

The consulting process derives from the consulting strains of its history. The *form* of the process is based on the scientific method/Operations Research framework. The *content* is based on behavioral mechanisms and interactive techniques for establishing and maintaining a client-consultant relationship. Both the technical and behavioral perspectives contribute to the execution of a complete consulting assignment.

There are some fundamental points to be noted about the consulting process:

- It is a general representation. The process fits consulting situations that are in the public or private sector, whether the issue is technical or managerial. The process reflects situations regardless of the type of contractual and management methods used.

- It is a multipurpose process. All steps in the process are not always carried out in the full manner presented. For instance, with certain types of behavioral issues, final reports are not usually written. Or if a consultant is called in to do only a feasibility study, an implementation plan may not be developed. Or perhaps the consultant rather than the client will initiate a consulting activity. The complete consulting process is detailed below, but it should be kept in mind that an individual assignment may not require all steps for its successful completion.
- The term "consultant," as used in this discussion, can also refer to the consultant team. Throughout the process, the word "consultant" refers to both the specific consultant responsible for the assignment and those supporting the consultant who are not part of the client group.

THE PROCESS OF CONSULTING

One of the first complete statements about the process of consulting was presented in an article by the social scientist and consultant Ronald Lippitt (1959). His view is that consulting is a relationship between client and consultant formed to work through change in the client organization. Dr. Lippitt identified seven phases to this end:

1. Development of the need for change
2. Establishment of a consulting relationship
3. Clarification of the client problem
4. Examination of alternative solutions and goals
5. Transformation of intentions into actual change efforts
6. Generalization and stabilization of a new level of functioning or group structure
7. Achievement of a terminal relationship with the consultant and a continuity of change

Twenty years later, this process was described with a slight change of emphasis by the political scientist and consultant Richard L. Pattenaude (1979). His formulation of the consulting process is comprised of these steps:

1. Recognition of the problem
2. Generation of solution strategies

3. Decision to seek a consultant
4. Specification of the problem
5. Search for a consultant
6. Selection of a consultant
7. Use of the consultant
8. Evaluation of the consultant's product
9. Integration of the consultant's product in the client organization
10. Evaluation of experience with consultant

Building upon these earlier articles, the process can now be defined as being comprised of the following stages:

1. *Issue Recognition* (recognizing the need for change). There is a tension within the environment of the client's organization which creates an issue. The issue is recognized by the client and appropriate measures are sought to resolve it. All possibilities are evaluated, including the option of using consultant services. If a decision is reached to use a consultant, appropriate and qualified firms or individuals are investigated.

2. *Consultant Selection*. A small number of experienced and knowledgeable consultants (within the client's organization or outside of it) are asked by the client to present their credentials and to discuss the organizational situation requiring their services.

The consultants are evaluated on their oral exchanges and their written proposals, which describe how to define, resolve, and implement changes in the situation. Usually one consultant is selected and asked to perform the services in a contractual framework.

3. *Engagement Beginning*. The consultant and client meet to refine the scope of the consulting activity. The logistics and communication patterns are established and needed resources are identified. The consultant meets the client's associates and resource people and becomes familiar with the organization. The proposal submitted by the consultant is reapproved, with any modifications by the client and with the recognition that they will work in concert with the goals and objectives of the organization.

4. *Issue Definition*. The consultant reviews the issue. He develops ways to unearth the root causes of the issue and presents this method to the client. Upon agreement by the client, the consultant then carries out the exploration. Interviews with relevant personnel, perusal of organizational documents and files, and collection of related external data help to define the issue. The findings from this endeavor are presented to the client. The subsequent responsibilities of client and consultant are discussed, and the resulting feedback may change the definition of the issue. The consultant seeks a mandate to look for ways of resolving the issue.

5. *Resolution Pathways.* Having clearly focused on the issue, the consultant now develops a set of alternatives for overcoming it. These alternatives are presented to the client, and are thoroughly examined and evaluated. From this interaction, the consultant and client formulate criteria for choosing a pathway(s) which could be most useful in dealing with the issue. The client then uses these criteria to select the best alternative(s).

6. *Pathway Implementation.* The consultant now generates mechanisms and a schedule for implementing the chosen alternative(s). The effort includes understanding what changes are needed and when they should be implemented. Implementation also involves outlining possible resistances to change and procedures for dealing with them, setting up a timetable, and presenting ways in which the changes can be integrated into the organizational environment. This implementation plan is then presented to the client, and after pertinent discussion and modification, it is approved.

7. *Monitoring and Termination.* The implementation plan is now put into effect. As new insights occur, they are incorporated into the plan. At this stage, the consultant composes and presents to the client a draft report of the consulting endeavor. The client reviews the draft copy, circulates it among the client group, and returns their comments to the consultant. These observations and critiques are incorporated into the report along with further results from the implementation. The consultant concurrently has reached agreement with the client on whether follow-up services are needed beyond the length of the original contract and under what conditions the consultant might provide such services. A final report is handed to the client soon thereafter, which concludes the basic service agreement.

8. *Evaluation and Follow-Up.* Shortly after contract termination, it is a fairly common practice for the consultant and client to do an internal evaluation. The consultant discusses with his peers the overall performance of the consulting team and what was learned from the experience. They discuss the strong and weak points of the assignment, including the tasks, interactions or presentations, and the prognosis for future consulting with the client. The client also evaluates the performance of the consultant, including how well the two people and groups got along, their satisfaction with the results, and whether the client might wish to engage the consultant in the future.

In the following seven chapters, each stage of this process will be dealt with in greater breadth and depth. Figure 3.1 presents the sequence of the consulting process. Under each step are the major topics covered in the following chapters. This figure serves as a handy guide to the consulting process and should be referred to often.

Issue Recognition
- Client awareness of issue
- Client decision to use a consultant

Consultant Selection
- Client/consultant meeting
- Proposals requested and developed
- Proposals submitted and evaluated
- Consultant(s) chosen and contract secured

Beginning the Engagement
- Client barriers and concerns
- Developing strategies for change

Issue Definition
- How to define an issue
- How to conduct an interview
- Types of data-gathering

Resolution Pathways
- How to give feedback
- How to conduct meetings
- Developing alternatives

Pathway Implementation
- Resistance to change
- Conflict Resolution
- Implementation Planning and Control

Termination and Evaluation
- Writing a report
- Performance evaluation
- Joint evaluation discussion
- Follow-up

Figure 3.1.   Stages of the Consulting Process

Case Example 3.1. Diary of a Consulting Assignment

February 21: I was called by the chief operating officer, Mr. Axet, of Over-Easy Housewares Company, who said his company was not performing well. Their productivity had dropped, and their employees were suffering feelings of malaise. He also stated that he wanted the company to diversify its activities. I said I'd be willing to come by to discuss these matters further, and we agreed to meet a week later.

February 28: Today I met with Mr. Axet. I presented the credentials of the consulting concern I represent, emphasizing our breadth of experience with diversifying company operations. I asked Mr. Axet whether he was reviewing some other consulting firms, and he replied that four other firms were being considered. The company is a small business that has been family owned since its founding 53 years ago. As he was telling me that he and his two sons are responsible for all major decisions, the telephone rang. While Axet was speaking to the caller, I quickly formulated an action strategy. We spent the last part of our 30-minute meeting discussing how my firm would create a tailored approach to building a more effective sales force, marketing strategy, and potential set of products to enhance the company's existing product line. We exchanged information and said a cordial good-bye.

March 15: I received a letter from Over-Easy offering congratulations for being chosen to "advise and assist with all necessary preparations for becoming a force in the marketplace." Axet and I scheduled a meeting of the major people to be involved from each firm for three days hence.

March 18: My team and Axet's team met in the conference lounge at Over-Easy's headquarters. Everyone was somewhat stiff during this first meeting. The diversification issue was again addressed, and we presented Pert and Gantt charts, the expected results, and the anticipated benefits to Over-Easy. The Axet family was impressed and gave us carte blanche to garner any necessary facts and viewpoints needed for the completion of the assignment.

March 25: My team set up interviews with various members of the Axet firm to uncover the perceived problems of the company. We talked with clerical and production staff, two production managers, the controller, the director of sales, and each Axet executive alone.

Our findings showed that each Axet family member had the same view: a stronger firm required a larger product line. The employees felt that expanding into new products was a worthy objective, once the existing "house" was put in order. They said the problems with the company were

- No incentives for advancement. Employees were discouraged by their perception of a management attitude toward promotion, which was that increasing proficiency in one's job was the only way to advance, rather than the opportunity to learn new skills.
- New products meant learning new techniques "by one and all, top to bottom," as one employee put it.
- Most employees had made Over-Easy their career and felt that any overnight transformations would be difficult to cope with and adjust to.

March 27: Back at the office, the team and I sat around struggling to define the root causes of the company's problem. It was hypothesized that the desire to diversify was really management's excuse for their failure to provide a more satisfying work environment. Thus, the proposed action was to lay out a marketing strategy for an increased product line as the guise for training the entire company in more effective communication, delegation of responsibility, incentives for advancement, and ways to enhance their job tasks.

March 31: Our consulting team met with the Axets and presented our marketing plan in detail. There was a flurry of discussion among the three men. At one point the youngest son asked, "Will the employees go for this plan with the same enthusiasm we have?" I replied that they would be enthused only if they were made to feel part of the operation. The three men looked somewhat surprised and said they were unsure that this approach would work. However, they agreed to give it a try. We expected the first phase to take about three months.

May 1: Over the last month, we have been conducting meetings, seminars, small-group sessions, and mini-courses on the projected impact of new products on the company. The response from the Axets and their employees has been positive. Last week, we sent around a confidential questionnaire asking what new products people would like to see as part of company operations, how they felt about their current jobs, how these products would affect what they were doing now, and whether they felt the preparation given to them by us was sufficient to handle the new products. The results we've obtained are surprising. It turns out that most of the employees feel better able to do their current jobs and have made many suggestions as to how their tasks could be made more interesting and satisfying. Some employees stated that the Axets needed to be retrained or should step aside. The responses also indicated that new products should be considered only after the employees had incorporated their job improvement skills into the execution of their current tasks.

May 5: I met with the Axets alone and discussed the questionnaire findings. All three men were speechless at first. Finally, the elder Axet mumbled, "If you can't take the heat, you'd better get out of the kitchen." This broke the ice, and they began to reconsider their positions. I said that if the new employee suggestions were implemented with monitoring, productivity in the existing product line could go up as a function of the increase in morale.

When both employees and management were ready, I reasoned, then the market plan could be put into effect. We agreed that my team would be retained through June to observe and evaluate the ability of the employees to use their suggestions. We would act as liaisons between the Axets and the company staff to iron out difficulties as they arose.

June 15: My consulting group has helped to integrate most of the employee suggestions within the company's operations. We were invited to a company picnic last Sunday and were pleased to see the improved interaction among everyone. We were pleasantly surprised at the gift which the company presented to us: a soap sculpture of the three "pure" monkeys (hear, see, and speak no evil). I finished a letter to the Axets offering to be "on call." We would provide services, I said, on a regular "checkup" basis to ensure the continuation of the company's improved health.

July 15: Today, we completed an internal review of the consulting assignment at Over-Easy. The team assessed the strong and weak points of our consulting activity.

Overall, we felt it was a positive experience.

December 1: Since the last entry, we've visited Over-Easy on seven occasions. The firm is now ready to reconsider diversifying and clearly would like to retain our services to help them do so.

It appears from this consultant's account of an assignment that the consulting process was creatively used to counter employee dissatisfactions so that the marketing plan could be implemented. The "proof of the pudding," however, is found in the second case example, later in this chapter.

REASONS FOR USING CONSULTANTS

"Anybody'd be crazy to bring in fancy-footed folks who would tell you what you already know" was part of a response to a consulting survey a few years ago. The view that consultants are unable to do more than restate the obvious has prevailed in spite of the growing use of consulting services. If, as the writer quoted here exclaimed, all they did was to cite the obvious, then at the very least, client time and money is being wasted. But a consultant needs more than just common sense to uncover the real issues in the complex and ambiguous client environment. The client needs a consultant who can

- Provide a custom-made process to resolve an issue troubling the client,
- Give an impartial perspective to the consulting assignment,
- Supply skills and resources on a short-term basis, and
- Draw upon past experience with similar issues (Kindred 1973; Gottfried 1969a; Haslett 1971; Hollander 1963; Shay 1974; Kubr 1976).

What is behind the apparently straightforward client need for objective, fast, and effective consulting services? It appears from studies, vignettes, and discussions with clients that the client's perception of the consultant *role* is the key to meeting their needs. There has been a fair amount written on the varying consulting roles. Yet, many books and articles often tend to overlook the context in which the roles are carried out.

A consultant role is defined by those characteristics which the consultant uses in developing the relationship with the client. Parkinson (1971) has likened consultants to bees that fly from enterprise to enterprise collecting the best experiences and then presenting these as their own "honey." Or the consultant could be cast as the Lone Ranger, coming quietly into the client's environment, working behind the scenes to catalyze change, and then riding off into the sunset (Ross 1977). A role implies a course of action usually defined by another occupation or profession. The dominant roles that are found in the consulting process are presented in table 3.1, which provides the primary and secondary characteristics of each role, along with references. Next, each role is related to the various stages of the consulting process in table 3.2. Each consultant role is presumed to exert a large influence in one or more stages of the consulting process.

Some roles have more positive effects than others in a successful consultation. *Issue Recognition* and *Monitoring and Termination* are the two stages that provide the best indicators of client satisfaction. As illustrated in table 3.2, only two roles, the *scientist* and the *broker*, have any impact in both of these stages. A client would be most likely to ask a consultant in either of these roles to recommend a consultant of like character. Also, the client would feel assured that any consultant subsequently chosen would carry out the process to completion. The other roles can exert a positive influence in some stages. In fact, in certain consulting assignments it may make sense to use one or more of these roles to accomplish any given stage of an assignment. In all roles a high level of consultant and client responsibility is required to successfully complete a consulting engagement.

What kinds of responsibility should be brought into the consulting process by the consultant and the client? Box 3.1 presents the range of attitudes with which the consultant or client may approach the assignment. Each point in the client column is reinforced by a respective perception or task in the consultant's column. It is not expected that clients or consultants always come to a new situation bearing all of these understandings. The next seven chapters will provide an understanding of such responsibilities as an integral part of the consulting activity.

Case Example 3.2. Diary of a Consulting Assignment (continued)

January 15: I received a call from Over-Easy today. Mr. Axet Sr. wants my team to work on giving the company more product for its dollar and

Table 3.1. Roles a Consultant Can Assume

Roles	Primary Characteristics	Secondary Characteristics	Sources
Doctor	Client realizes something is amiss in his organizational environment; calls in consultant to diagnose situation and prescribe cure.	Consultant is hired to do something for the client. Consultant offers little assistance in implementing resolution	Margulies, *Conceptual Foundations of Organizational Development,* 1978, chapter 5; McGill, *Organizational Development for Operating Managers,* 1977, chapter 3.
	Consultant performs the process with mini-client interaction and offers possible resolutions.	If resolution is difficult to implement, consultant recommends another consultant for advice.	Schein, *Process Consultation: Its Role in Organizational Development,* 1969, chapter 1; Tilles, "Understanding the Consultant's Role," *Harvard Business Review,* Nov./Dec. 1961, pp. 87–99.
	Client is expected to follow resolution pathway.		
Marketer	Consultant attempts to sell client packaged services.	Consultant has little interaction with client or client staff.	Margulies, *Conceptual Foundations of Organizational Development,* 1978, chapter 3.
	Consultant wants to establish image for client. Consultant tailors resolution to fit client image.	Consultant is more interested in producing report than implementing resolution.	McGill, *Organizational Development for Operating Managers,* 1977, chapter 3; Schein, *Process Consultation: Its Role in Organizational Development,* 1969, chapter 1; Tilles, "Understanding the Consultant's Role," *Harvard Business Review,* Nov./Dec. 1961, pp. 87–99.

Role			
Scientist	Consultant acts as catalyst for change. Consultant observes and reflects on issue in objective manner. Consultant follows step-by-step process toward resolution of issue.	Consultant works only on issue given by client. Consultant's forte is overcoming barriers encountered in consulting process. Consultant interacts only to resolve issue.	Steele, *Consulting for Organizational Change*, 1975, chapter 5; G. Lippitt, *Organizational Renewal*, 1969, chapter 4.
Detective	Emphasis is on gathering evidence to resolve issue "puzzle." Consultant's forte is vaguely defined issues; has little influence in implementing resolution to issue.	Consultant is equally facile with ideas and people. Consultant is able to uncover unusual insights. Consultant interacts only to examine issue.	Steele, *Consulting for Organizational Change*, 1975, chapter 5; van de Vliet, "The Organizational Consultant: Controller? Pilot? Coach?" *SAM Adv. Mgmt. Jrnl.*, July 1971, pp. 19–26.
Expert Consultant	Consultant has the latest widest knowledge about client issue. Consultant advocates a course of action to resolve issue. Generally, work is complete before implementation stage begins.	Knows what is best for client. Generally, consultant is strong on technical approach and weak on behavioral approach. Consultant is usually contacted by client.	G. Lippitt, *Organizational Renewal*, 1969, chapter 4.
Broker	Client and consultant share equal responsibility for resolving issue.	Results produced are implemented before final report is complete.	Margulies, *Conceptual Foundations of Organizational Development*, 1978, chapter 5; McGill, *Organizational Development for Operating Managers*, 1977, chapter 3. Schein, *Process Consultation: Its Role in Organizational Development*, 1969, chapter 1.
	There is joint participation in decision making, with client responsible for final decision. Consultant helps client develop skills for defining and resolving future issues.	Consultant interacts with client in each stage of the consulting process. Success is based on a high level of client satisfaction and consultant performance.	G. Lippitt, *Organizational Renewal*, 1969, chapter 4.

(continued)

Table 3.1. (*continued*)

Roles	Primary Characteristics	Secondary Characteristics	Sources
Sanitary Engineer	Consultant assists in maintaining status quo. Consultant produces results which suggest making no substantive changes. Consultant would help in delaying any client decisions.	Consultant could be used as mouthpiece of client. Consultant could be scapegoat or whipping boy if organizational situation worsens. Consultant has no client impetus for resolving issue.	Hollander, *Business Consultants and Clients*, 1963, introduction.

Table 3.2. Roles and the Consulting Process

	Consulting Roles						
Process Stages	Doctor	Marketer	Scientist	Detective	Expert Consultant	Broker	Sanitary Engineer
Issue Recognition	S		S		S	S	—
Consultant Selection	—	L	—	L	L	—	—
Engagement Beginning	L	S	L	S	S	S	S
Issue Definition	S	S	L	L	L	S	S
Resolution Pathways	L	L	L	L	L	L	S
Pathway Implementation	S	S	S	S	S	L	—
Monitoring and Termination	—	S	S	—	—	L	—
Evaluation and Follow-Up	—	—	S	—	—	S	S

KEY: L = large impact; S = small impact; — = no impact.

Box 3.1. Client and Consultant Responsibilities in the Consulting Process

Client

- Committed to change
- Willing to trust consultant
- Open to learning new skills and feel comfortable practicing them
- Aware of the nature of the consulting process
- Willing to be the decision maker
- Able to openly discuss the current state of the organization and the issue of concern with the consultant
- Willing to provide the consultant with requested information in an expedient fashion
- Desirous of informing the consultant of any project changes
- Prepared to effectively evaluate and critique the consultant's activity
- Willing to continue monitoring the changes made in the organization and call back the consultant for assistance as needed
- Willing to learn how to define and correct issues of the organizational environment

Consultant

- Committed to helping create an environment where change can occur
- Willing to interact in a mutually supportive way with the client
- Skilled at helping client group accept and support organizational changes
- Proficient at transmitting information about consulting
- Able to listen sensitively and empathize with the client
- Able to carry out the consulting assignment in an efficient and punctual manner
- Motivated to complete the consulting process in an ethically sincere way
- Capable of creating an interactive environment in which feedback is given and conflicts are dealt with
- Open to giving the client additional help as the need arises
- Able to use the changes that result from an assignment to improve working relationships in the consultant group or organization

then more profit for its products. I rounded up the same crew and off we went to increase their fortune and ours.

January 18: We went out to Over-Easy to meet with the Axets, the controller, the marketing manager, and the production managers. They were cordial and willing to listen to what we had to say. We presented them with the marketing strategy (which we had previously developed) straightforwardly. My team discussed what the responsibilities of all participants would be in the market strategy implementation. There was some discussion about whether we would be able to accomplish all assigned tasks within the given time frame, but everyone agreed to do his best.

January 31: We have been constructing a detailed decision framework for choosing new product ventures and have been doing cost-benefit analyses of some ventures that are likely prospects. Today, we had a meeting with the client group to present our findings.

The clients and their staff sat quietly while we explained the decision framework and showed them how they could gather the data necessary for choosing new products. The meeting ended with the controller remarking, "If this scheme puts us in the red, it could undermine all of our business to date."

February 15: We had completed a sample decision framework, which we showed to Mr. Axet Sr. He was impressed, noting that productivity in the firm had never been at a higher level, nor had sales been better. He said that we should give copies to his sons and that we should be there when they made the "big decisions."

March 5: At the quarterly directors' meeting, the three Axets and our team were present. With our deliberations being recorded, the Axets and we chose the new products to be included in their production line. Over beers at lunch, the oldest son remarked, "Dad, the future has really never looked better at Over-Easy. In large part, we have this consulting team to thank."

March 25: We have been away from Over-Easy since the 5th, putting together the logistics and costs of the new products as well as assessing the likely impacts of the new production activities on the old product line. In the early afternoon I got a call from the controller whose voice sounded tense as he spoke: "Look, you guys are seen by the family as the best thing since sliced bread. They'd trust you to do almost anything for them. But I feel you may be taking us on a train ride over a cliff. Not once have you mentioned how the sales effort will be upgraded in order to support distribution of the new products. And what about the increased staff needed to produce the products? Do you have any idea how much capital investment will be required? How will it be amortized? What kinds of profit projections are you making? I need to know answers to these questions before I can justify any kind of increase in expenditures, or negotiate for any loans that will be required." I calmly explained that our financial analysis was almost finished, and we would have those answers for him by the end of the week.

March 28: I met alone with the controller and explained the financial posture we had developed for this undertaking. After two and one-half hours, he seemed satisfied that "the venture will fly, if we invest prudently." I sent a memo to the Axets summarizing the meeting.

April 20: We again met with the principal staff and the Axets to iron out the logistical details. As we were concluding the meeting, the conference door swung open, and in walked a group of employees, most of whom we had interviewed initially. They quietly stood near the door while their spokeswoman, Marilyn Remache, presented the Axets with a petition, signed by the majority of the employees, which protested that the new product development plan was proceeding without their input. The petition called for an employee representative to become immediately involved in the decision-making process, for the decisions already made to be reconsidered with the employee representative present, and for delegation of responsibility to the employees and their representative in implementing the product development plan. The Axets were shocked by this occurrence, the management staff was snickering at the turn of events, and the employees were adamant about having their demands met. The meeting broke up with Axet Sr. grasping the petition and saying, "At 9 a.m. tomorrow I want to see my staff, your staff [pointing to me], and our employee representative in my office."

April 21: We all met in Axet's office. We were anxious and uncertain about the outcome. Axet did most of the talking. He recognized the unmet demands of the employees, agreed to include the employee representative in decisions affecting the entire company, and agreed to pay particular attention to the impact of new product production on the employees. The meeting was then adjourned. Axet Sr. said he wanted to speak with me privately. We went into an anteroom where he explained his disappointment in me and my team's insensitivity to the needs of *his* employees. He said that his trust in my abilities had been sorely undermined, but that one big goof did not wipe out the positive things we had done for him. He suggested we go back and incorporate his workers into our plans for him.

April 28: We sent the Axets a rough draft of the product development plan. It was reviewed that afternoon.

July 2: We have been working closely with the controller to implement the plan and to develop a sales staff. Today we made a presentation to the delayed quarterly directors' meeting, at which the management staff and the employees' representative were also present. The delivery was received with stone silence. The employee representative then presented some observations which she had gathered. It turns out, she said, that productivity, worker morale, satisfaction with management, willingness to make Over-Easy a career, and opportunities for skills development had all decreased markedly since January. Furthermore, the suggestion mechanism set up a year ago by the consultants had broken down. She summed up the situation by pointing at me and saying, "You have created a monster!" I said we would get right to work modifying our plan to incorporate these factors.

July 15: I received a phone call from Axet Sr. thanking me for my services, but stating that they were no longer desired. He suggested that we meet in a different context some time in the future.

This case example shows a breakdown in communications. Had the consultant been aware of employee dissatisfaction sooner, the failure of the entire project probably could have been avoided. No stone should be left unturned by the consultant in the quest for information. The viability of any proposed issue resolution depends on its acceptance by those who will be directly affected by it. Their needs and possible resistance to change must be considered and dealt with if the assignment is not to collapse, as it did in this case.

REVIEW AND EXTENSION

The reasons for retaining consultants are easily understood once the stages of the consulting process are identified. After a decision is made to obtain outside services, the choice of consultant is based upon the role the consultant will play in the client organization. Those roles that allow for the greatest flexibility in dealing with a client are most apt to be successful (G. Lippett 1972). From the steps in the consulting process and the various roles a consultant may assume, the responsibilities of both client and consultant are drawn. These are the guideposts by which progress is measured along the consulting process pathway. By carefully examining results and expectations at each step along the way, the consultant and client move toward a more precise definition and resolution of the issue. This process of examination and feedback also promotes the kind of trusting cooperation that goes a long way toward preventing the innumerable misunderstandings that can arise as a result of poor communication. The following chapters discuss the components of the consulting process in greater detail.

Chapter 4

Securing the Engagement

OVERVIEW

Most experienced consultants say that securing the engagement is an art best understood by instinct. Although the skills needed to win a client assignment can be learned in the environment of the consultant's group, they rarely are. Most frequently, they are obtained by actual practice, and indeed, a true proficiency in the art requires experience that can be obtained in no other way. By understanding what to expect in such a situation, the consultant can arm himself with the knowledge and strategies needed to secure an engagement, before actually entering the arena. This chapter seeks to prepare the consultant with those skills by presenting the sequential cycle that is representative of consultant-client matching.

The cycle begins with the client decision to use a consultant. Next, the consultant is contacted by the client, and in turn, this consultant prepares for the first meeting between the two. This process is detailed below, including the problems of consultant entry into the client organization and the client perception of the need for the consultant. Both the client and consultant do follow-up evaluations of the meeting to decide whether they can work together. The client probably screens a number of consultants and narrows the consultant candidates. From the chosen candidates, the client requests a response, usually a proposal. If the consultant is still interested, a proposal is written and submitted in the time frame specified by the client.

The consultant proposals are evaluated by the client in a variety of ways. This chapter will illustrate the evaluation methods. If the client wishes to have oral as well as written presentations from the consultant, another client-consultant meeting might be scheduled.

After all consultants' inputs are known to the client and the evaluation is complete, then the winner(s) of the job are selected. Subsequently, the contract is negotiated and signed by all parties. The full sequence of events may not occur in every case. For instance, in social work consulting, informal agreements, verified by a handshake or a letter, are common (Kadushin 1977). But, not taking any shortcuts in the contracting process can help to define the content of the consulting assignment by specifying the responsibilities of both parties.

CLIENT DECISION TO USE A CONSULTANT

A consultant is a resource of last resort. Once a potential client recognizes that there is an issue requiring immediate and effective action, in-house capabilities are first surveyed. If the necessary abilities to focus on the issue are not present, either because of personnel limitations or other priorities for staff time, then the client assesses other options. If procuring the services of a consultant seems to be the best alternative, then the prospective client seeks out and secures such services. Figure 4.1 demonstrates the initial evaluation process of the issue used to determine the need for a consultant. Note that the findings here are likely to evolve as a consultant is selected and the issue(s) tackled (see chapter 6). We shall examine the impetus and actions of those involved in forming a consultant-client bond. This examination will be slower and broader than the real-world situations one might encounter, in order to fully understand the origins of a consulting assignment and the motivations of both consultant and client.

Once the need for a consultant is recognized, the potential client assesses his knowledge of consulting. The client seeks answers to the following questions:

1. What kinds of consulting resources are available, and what are their capabilities?
2. How do I choose a consultant?
3. How do we work together, and what are my responsibilities in our interaction (Fisher 1967)?

Collecting this information requires the support of other organizational members. Together they create a procedure for using consulting advice. The procedure is also influenced by upper management's attitude toward the use of consultants, by the initial resistances of the client group, and by

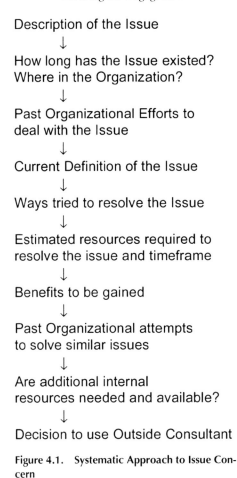

Description of the Issue
↓
How long has the Issue existed?
Where in the Organization?
↓
Past Organizational Efforts to
deal with the Issue
↓
Current Definition of the Issue
↓
Ways tried to resolve the Issue
↓
Estimated resources required to
resolve the issue and timeframe
↓
Benefits to be gained
↓
Past Organizational attempts
to solve similar issues
↓
Are additional internal
resources needed and available?
↓
Decision to use Outside Consultant

Figure 4.1. Systematic Approach to Issue Concern

the client's own biases (Waterbow 1970). This procedure results in a set of guidelines that will direct the consultant proposal and selection activities. Box 4.1 shows a sample of such guidelines.

While these guidelines are being formulated, the client is compiling a list of consultant candidates. One way the client may approach this is to solicit background information on consulting firms that are selected from referrals, general reputation, or prior experiences with the client organization. The client calls or writes each concern for information about the range of services they can provide, facilities, general experience related to the issue at hand, types of administrative, technical, and organizational skills, and other pertinent factors. From the responses of about a dozen firms (plus any internal resources available, such as an internal consultant group or any prospective new employees), an initial screening

Box 4.1. Client's Checklist for Soliciting Consultants

1. Has a procedure been followed for accessing the type of consulting resources desired?
2. Has personal contact been made between client and consultant?
3. What kind of information has been gained by meeting with each consultant? What are other organizational members' perceptions of each consultant?
4. How does the consultants' input modify the proposal—either its scope of work or its projected cost?
5. What kind of follow-up is done by the consultants, and what influence does this have on their subsequent proposal submissions?
6. Is there a need for an additional oral presentation by any of the consultants? Why?
7. How will the consultants' efforts be evaluated?
8. Do the contract negotiations reflect technical and professional compatibility between the selected consultant and our organization?

occurs. The purpose of this screening is to narrow the choices to three to five consultant candidates (ACEC 1976). At this time, the client group could also set a preliminary budget for this activity. The candidates are informed that they are being considered by the client organization, they are briefed on the issue, and then they are asked for an indication of interest. For each firm that expresses interest, a meeting is arranged between their representatives and representatives of the client organization. Any potential internal consultants would also be interviewed and evaluated in a similar manner.

FIRST CLIENT-CONSULTANT MEETING

The first meeting between the client and consultant is one of the most important in the consulting process. Here the initial impressions of consultant and client are formulated.

The client receives, for the first time, some objective reactions to the issue. The client and consultant begin to develop a sense of whether they can work together to resolve the issue.

Both client and consultant are seeking certain explicit and implicit things from the meeting. The client wants to know the nature of the consultant's resources, the constraints on using them, and how they would be used to deal with the issue. The consultant wants to determine whether he has the ability and desire to help, and what working for the client would entail. Both want to find out whether a compatible relationship can develop. The client and consultant preparation for the meeting, the actual meeting, and the respective follow-ups after the meeting are all integral parts of the mutual evaluation that is taking place.

The client's meeting preparation consists of three actions:

1. Briefing all relevant people within the organization on the intention to use a consulting service. The purpose of the briefing is to encourage the airing of reservations about the employment of a consultant.
2. Writing a succinct description of the issue.
3. Scheduling the meetings of all consultant candidates in close succession so that comparisons can be made on an equal basis.

The consultant's preparation for this meeting will be more extensive than the client's since the former must start from scratch to develop a preliminary understanding of the client's situation. There are two aspects to this preparation—the systematic and the psychological.

The systematic groundwork consists of first finding out the basic characteristics of the organization. This can be accomplished by referring to any number of documented sources. If possible, a brief history of the organization, its goals and functions, and any current incidents or events directly related to the issue inside or outside the organization should be unearthed. In addition, the consultant should contact any professional sources who might have insights into the organization (potential client) (Hunt 1977). Second, from the limited communication with the client, the consultant pieces together the broad framework of the issue by asking the following questions:

- Does the client or the organization have an issue? If so, what is it?
- What resources can I bring to bear to resolve this issue?
- What client constraints will limit the use of these resources?
- Is this an issue which, if I am not able to resolve alone, I can resolve through use of other consulting services? If so, which services would I consider?
- Is this a potential consulting assignment that could further the goals and objectives of the consulting firm (R. Lippett 1959; Gottfried 1969b)?

These questions can be discussed among the consulting group. Third, the consultant creates a presentation for the client based on responses to these questions. The answers to the above questions would also help the consultant decide how to approach the client.

The psychological considerations are oriented toward providing an interactive environment in which the client can have confidence in his own abilities as well as respect for the consultant's. That is, the client's self-image "is not jeopardized when he can declare that what he is lacking is something he need not (or should not) be expected to have in the first place, such as a specialized knowledge or technical competence outside his area of competence or expertise" (Bergen 1970, 399). The consultant should respect the client's wishes for confidentiality and exhibit a willingness to work with the client as a peer in a noncompetitive fashion. The consultant will seek not to gain influence, but to insure that the client's authority as decision maker is upheld. In essence, the consultant wants to be candid and compatible with the client and client group. The fundamental objective is to create a climate in which change can be considered and achieved (Robbins 1970). However, "unless there is some mutual consensus as to how the participants in the interaction perceive the purpose, direction and nature of the consultation, and how they will proceed together to achieve these objectives, the consultation is not likely to be effective" (Kadushin 1977, 146).

The development of this "mutual consensus" is the objective of the client-consultant meeting. Ideally, there is an equal exchange of knowledge and perceptions that clarifies each party's position in the other's mind. The meeting provides gut-level indications to each: for the client, whether or not the consultant has the professional competence and experience to carry out the assignment; for the consultant, whether or not the client has an issue amenable to resolution through the consultant's resources and what benefits are likely to result. Also, both parties have access to other colleagues who are capable of recognizing characteristics of the assignment that the consultant or client alone may miss.

In the debriefing session, each side evaluates the information gained and the compatibility of the potential relationship. The client assesses any changes in his understanding of the issue because of the interaction, the consultant's abilities and resources, the quality and timeliness of the likely results, and any consultant/client shortcomings. The consultant decides if he has the ability and desire to perform the consulting assignment and if the probable outcome will enhance his understanding and experience. He tries to ascertain whether a viable working relationship can be established with the client, if the client is sincere about wanting to deal with the situation, if the timing is right for the consultation, and if he (the consultant) has the necessary staff to carry out the project. The upshot of the debriefing is the client's decision—whether or not to ask the consultant to submit a project proposal—and the consultant's decision of whether or not to respond (Zaltman 1977). This sequence assumes a personal dynamic interchange between consultant and client which may not always be the case. For example, client solicitations might go to selected consultants based on firm specifications. Or, one meeting of all interested consultants could be held to clarify the scope of the work. Nevertheless, the one-on-one initial interaction is a crucial step in establishing rapport between a consultant and client, and the consequences of skipping or modifying this stage should be carefully considered.

SPECIAL TOPIC: THE CONSULTANT AS A PERSON

It is essential that a consultant possess certain personal qualities and capacities if he is to be an effective facilitator of organizational change (Rogers 1961; Dinkmeyer 1973). Some of these qualities are

- An ability to accept people for who they are and be empathetic toward their situation,
- The willingness to relate to clients on an individual basis,
- The sensitivity to reflect the client's positive attributes, helping him to feel competent and self-assured in the consultant's presence,
- The capability to establish a consultant-client relationship characterized by mutual trust and respect,
- The patience to work through client (and sometimes client-consultant) barriers in order to resolve the client issue,
- The motivation to deal with the client issue in a creative and adaptive manner,
- The courage to admit mistakes and use them as learning experiences, and
- The belief that the resolution to the client issue won't be perfect, but that it will be a realistic one that has emerged from the best efforts of client and consultant.

In sum, the consultant is concerned with people, seeing them as a mirror of himself: that is, able, dependable, friendly, helpful, and internally motivated. The consultant is concerned with the issue and thinks of the resolution process as a positive experience for both himself and the client. The process of resolving the issue is given the same weight as the resolution itself (Rogers 1961).

Case Example 4.1. The Anatomy of an Encounter

The Puritan Adoption Agency was having problems that were causing increasing concern to Mary Chireford, the director of services. Their turnover of professional staff was at an all-time high, with no abatement in sight. She knew what the problem was: Puritan's policy of rigorously screening homes in an effort to place children in suitable home environments. Although their 100-year-old reputation for sensitivity to the needs of the children and the families was based upon this policy, it was apparent that it was the cause of a growing restlessness among the staff over Puritan's definition of a proper home environment. Most of the staff felt that Puritan had not changed with the times, and that their requirements were restrictive and discriminatory, particularly their policy of dealing only with white children and families.

Chireford realized she had a dilemma on her hands. If she continued to uphold Puritan's policy, her clientele (mostly wealthy whites whose teenagers have had children out of wedlock) would remain, but her staff would leave. If she broadened the agency policy, the staff might stay, but her clientele might go elsewhere.

Determined to resolve this dilemma, she called in some child-care consultants to speak with her and the staff representatives. Two consultants came and went quickly; they seemed to have lots of ready-made ideas, but had difficulty relating them to Puritan's situation. A third firm, At Ease, Inc., was contacted, and their representative, Joe Assur, came to a prearranged meeting at Puritan. He walked into the conference room, met Chireford and the staff members, and sat down. Assur noticed reproductions of various Monet paintings on the walls. Before Chireford began the meeting, he commented on his affection for Monet's work and mentioned that he had visited the gardens at Giverny to see the water lilies that Monet had painted. Chireford responded with delight at his interest, saying how much she enjoyed Monet's work and how much of an inspiration it was to her. Two of the staff members echoed those sentiments.

Moving away from the painting, Assur proceeded to describe the sense of wonderment children have about the world and how this wonderment knows no racial or cultural bounds. "Watching children at play makes you realize that any child has the creative potential to become a great artist," he commented. He then asked what changes everyone thought were needed at the agency. Chireford and her staff opened up to Assur and were candid and firm in their responses. "What would you expect to happen if changes were not made?" he inquired next. After some strong replies, Assur said, "The issue here is not how to sustain revenue; it is how to get along with each other. I certainly can do a study to show what changes in agency revenue will result from serving a broader clientele. Yet, whatever my findings, the frayed relationships between the staff and Ms. Chireford must come first. Because without the ability to work together, the operations of the agency will suffer."

Chireford and staff agreed that the issue had to be resolved on two fronts—the policy changes and the ways of relating. Assur agreed to work with them in both areas, but under one condition: that they be willing to accept full responsibility for their part in resolving the issue.

The Puritan staff was pleased with his approach, told him so, and let him know that they would be in touch within the week to arrange for a proposal submission.

This example, which is continued later in the chapter, points out the importance of initial client contact with the consultant. In this case, effective use of an entry motif created a congenial atmosphere that was conducive to interaction.

CLIENT'S DECISION TO REQUEST PROPOSALS

From the outcome of the client-consultant meetings, the client now decides which consultants should submit proposals (including external and internal consultants). The client writes up the statement of the issue and the proposed effort to resolve it. This statement is mailed to all chosen consultants. It asks the consultant to submit a technical proposal and a cost proposal (for the specified payment scheme). Those consultants not chosen by the client should receive a notice to this effect. Each prospective consultant then reads through the proposal statement and decides, based on the statement and previous contact with the client, whether he is willing and able to respond. As a courtesy to the client, the prospective consultant should inform the client in writing as soon as possible if he decides not to submit a proposal.

CONSULTANT COMPOSES AND SUBMITS A PROPOSAL

Once the consultant has agreed to respond to the client solicitation, the task of creating a technical and cost proposal begins. There are four elements to bear in mind to produce a proposal of merit:

1. *Perspective*. This element is generated by a careful reading and discussion of the solicitation. The following questions should be kept in mind:

What is the essence of the issue?
What would the client like to do about the issue?
What approaches can be taken to writing the proposal?
What approach might other proposers use? How can we do better?
Has anything like the proposed effort been done before? Can we get the appropriate documentation?
What advantages do we have in responding to this client solicitation?
What disadvantages do we have? How can we overcome them?
Are there any cost-cutting factors that we can include in the proposal?
How can the material in the proposal be presented most effectively?

How will our proposal improve the client's situation? Are these the
results we want to strive for?

Answering these questions will enable resources to be collected, the
proposal to be outlined, and the writing to commence (Bermont 1979).

2. *Form.* There are two formats that can be followed in organizing the
proposal. They are the *flowchart* and the *response matrix* (Holtz 1979). The
flowchart enables the communicator to group the ideas of the technical
approach in a logical manner for rapid comprehension.

Figure 4.2 is an example of such a flowchart. If the figure is read from
top to bottom, each statement answers the implied question "why?" that
is introduced by the preceding statement. If the figure is read from bottom to top, each statement answers the implied question "how?" that is
introduced by the succeeding task. The response matrix is used as an in-

Why?	Literature Search	How?
↓	Determine which concepts to emphasize	↑
↓	Give historical precedent for using selected concepts	↑
↓	Relate concepts to client issue	↑
↓	Define client issue	↑
↓	Generate possible alternative pathways to issue resolution	↑
↓	Discuss constraints to each pathway	↑
↓	Select preferred pathway(s)	↑
↓	Define consultant role	↑
↓	Define client role	↑
↓	Discuss viability of expected results	↑

Figure 4.2.   Sample Flowchart of a Technical Approach to a Proposal

ternal aid to cross-reference the items in the proposal. Each proposal item is listed in one column. Across the page the resources required and time frame are given for each item. The matrix can be used to create an outline of the technical approach and can serve as a checklist to ensure that each proposal item has been addressed.

3. *Emphasis.* The style of the proposal should be low key, factual, and noninflative.

The tone of the proposal should be enthusiastic and realistic. The emphasis of the proposal should be on establishing credibility. A client or evaluator could approach the proposal with an attitude that could be anywhere along the following spectrum:

- "Never heard of you, but I don't like your name or the fact that you're a stranger to us. You're going to have to show me."
- "You're entitled to your day in court. I'll read what you have to say and I hope it's good."
- "Ho-hum, hope this one isn't as dull as the last one."
- "I know this outfit, and they have a good reputation. This ought to be a decent proposal."
- "Hmmm. This looks like a pretty strong outfit. This could be promising."

These initial attitudes will either entrench or change as the reading proceeds (Holtz 1979). To ensure that the reader makes up his own mind in a favorable manner, the consultant must do three things:

1. Gain attention. The beginning of the report should entice the reader into a complete reading by providing a compelling and lively introduction to the ideas that follow.
2. Arouse interest. Focus the client's attention on special methods or contributions of the proposal and describe the potential benefits of the results.
3. Turn interest into conviction. Create a desire to use these consulting services by presenting the scope of work in realistic, logical terms. The objective is not to compare the consultant's services with others, but to concretely and succinctly build the case for using this consultant.

Together, these creative attributes will act to establish proposal credibility with the client.

4. *Strategy.* This element consists of reading between the lines of the solicitation to understand what the hidden agendas are, if any, and what the client's biases are likely to be.

Box 4.2.   Checklist for Proposal Submission

Item	Elements
Transmittal letter	• Does it accurately summarize the proposed effort and its predicted results?
Proposal graphics	• Does the cover catch the eye and reflect the tone of the proposal? • Is it bound neatly and are separate sections readily accessible?
Proposal contents	• Are all sections properly labeled? • Is there a table of contents, list of illustrations, or acknowledgments (if needed)?
Abstract	• Is there a clear and concise summary of the proposal?
Proposal body	• Is the proposal organized in an effective manner, and does it clearly address the issues raised in the proposal request? • Have all specifications been responded to? • Have a consistent writing style and graphics and typing format been used?
Introduction	• Is the stage properly set? • Are the causes of the current situation presented? • Have past attempts to deal with the situation been noted?
Technical approach	• Is the approach clearly defined and simply but logically developed? • Have graphics been used to augment the textual portion? • Have the results been clearly explained? • Have the benefits and shortcomings to using the method presented been delimited?
Management plan	• Are all required charts and information about the proposer's resources included? • Have the consultant's relevant experience and overall qualifications been cogently presented? • Has the plan been specifically tailored to this effort?
Appendices/costs	• Has all "filler" been identified and removed? • Are they consistent with proposed resources? • Are they all accounted for, utilizing a payment scheme chosen by the consultant or client? • Are they competitive?

Some likely "trouble spots" to be on the alert for: those who have worked for the client in the past, the issue's relation to the overall concerns of the organization, and areas where costs can be reduced. Discovering how the proposal will be evaluated and by whom, and agency policies regarding the solicitation (such as punctuality of submission, stress on low bidder, reluctance to use new consultants, etc.) will further orient the proposal. The key here is to find advantages that can be capitalized upon to reduce costs and/or increase technical competitiveness.

A proposal checklist is presented in box 4.2, which outlines another, equally acceptable way of producing a quality and winning proposal (Holtz 1979).

PROPOSALS ARE EVALUATED AND
CONSULTANT(S) SELECTED

After the client has received all submissions, the time-consuming effort of finding the best candidate (or candidates) to do the job begins. The procedure involves the following:

1. Evaluation preparations. This consists of forming a review committee that will evaluate the technical merits of each proposal. This committee generally reviews the submissions apart from their cost portions so as not to unduly bias their objectivity. The committee consists of members from inside and/or outside the client organization who have prior knowledge of the issue, but who generally have little knowledge of or exposure to the prospective consultants.

2. Evaluation. The committee decides what criteria will be used to evaluate the proposals and the relative weight of each factor. These decisions form the objective yardstick by which a winner will be selected. Evaluations can be made with fair objectivity or with overt biases, and the consultant's proposal should reflect his understanding of the committee's likely attitude. Most evaluations have criteria matched to a maximum amount of points. The "score" for each evaluation is the sum of the weightings for the criteria. An example can be found in table 4.1.

The committee carefully reads the proposals and arrives at a consensus of an overall score for each. These scores are returned to the client. The client could then choose the winner(s) based on technical competence alone. More likely, he will incorporate the proposal price into the evaluation. (Many times, if internal consulting is available, the client will use their costs as a minimum from which to judge all outside responses. If the internal consultants are competitive also, then there may be no contest.)

3. Follow-up. If the client knows how much he is willing to spend to resolve the issue, then this figure can be compared with the submitted cost

Table 4.1.   Evaluation Criteria Scores

Criteria	Weighting (Points)
Understanding of the issue	40
Validity and practicality of the approach	20
Organization experience and qualifications	20
Availability and competence of staff	20
Total	100

proposals. Another meeting could be held with those consultants whose proposals got high technical scores to negotiate the scope of the work and its cost. The client's objective is to find a highly qualified proposer at the right price. The client may not wish to choose the least expensive bid, because the results per evaluation point could be lower than with other proposers. This choice could actually result in costing the client more in the long run.

Along with the technical and cost evaluations, the impressions of the client group and the consultant's references are figured in. The client is looking for someone whose integrity and capability can be trusted (Shay 1974; Hunt 1977). All other things being equal, the client tends to choose the consultant whose personality and operating style best fit his own (more will be said on this later). Considering all factors, the client chooses the winner(s) and notifies him and the other candidates by mail. As with any part of the consulting process, these three steps can be modified as the client organization sees fit.

CONTRACT NEGOTIATED AND SIGNED

The contract is essentially the proposal, with a few extra items, including the following:

- The duration for which the contract is in effect
- A clause for renewing or extending the contract
- The contract cancellation procedure
- The means for arbitrating any contract dispute
- The method and schedule of billing by the consultant
- The client responsibilities
- Any special provisions

There are different types of contracts that can be drawn up to suit the needs of the client, but they should all contain the above elements. Variations include a onetime, one-day voucher, an intermittent series of tasks of fixed or varying duration over a year, a continuous two-year effort, or an initial contract with a series of renewals (G. Lippett 1978; Shenson 1980).

Another important although often non-articulated element in the agreement between consultant and client is a mutual will to work together to achieve the objectives of the consultation through consensus and with respect for each other. At each stage of the consulting assignment, their working relationship should be open to review, criticism, and, if necessary, modification (AMA 1977). Once a trusting relationship is established, both client and consultant will find it easier to take risks and institute changes (Goodstein 1978; Argyris 1965). Once again, the dynamic process of change is, after all, the essence of consulting.

Case Example 4.2. Proposing: Is It the Same as Engagement?

To continue from case example 4.1, Joe Assur returned to his firm, At Ease, Inc., feeling confident that he had established a respectful rapport with the people at the Puritan Adoption Agency. Assur and his staff proceeded to assemble the parts of an unrequested proposal. In the proposal briefing, Assur at one point stressed "the sincere willingness of our client to consider seriously what we give them. So it had better be good!" The proposal they produced was really two proposals in one, since there were two technical approaches to the client issue. One approach was a proposal for increasing staff influence in the agency operations. The second plan was for attracting a wider range of customers. Included with each was a sample means of implementing the tasks, and the time frame for it. A synopsis of the firm's past experience and the consulting team members' abilities was also included. A budget proposal was submitted separate from, but accompanying, the technical approaches.

Assur, as team leader, decided that the budget for either approach would be the same. This way, he reasoned, the choice of consulting services would be based on need, not on cost. Over the course of his consulting career, Assur had developed a "devil's advocate" style of presenting a proposal. In the approach narrative, he used a Socratic motif to present and then question each idea. For instance, a portion of the proposal narrative for option one, increasing staff influence, read as follows:

> The stakeholder theory. This theory simply says that employees should have a larger stake in the governance and direction of the firm they work in (not for). That is, each employee is potentially a holder of decision-making power which can exert influence upon the management of the company. Why should this be? After all, most employees are satisfied with good

wages, a comfortable working environment, and a chance for advancement. Or are they? Studies have shown that there are really two basic factors that influence situations requiring a stakeholder approach to management: peer group pressure and group job satisfaction. It has been found that the stronger the employees bond together socially, the more the employee voice will be heard through this group. Conversely, with little group cohesion, employee demands tend to he articulated individually or in pairs. Second, peer group pressure is a force far stronger than any management edict. If the group wants more control over its vocational life, the forces brought to bear on management can be significant. This indicates that management must take the pulse of the employees to find out if these informal groups are advocating more control, before instituting any changes that will affect them directly. Managers frequently make the mistake of assuming their prior understanding of prevailing attitudes is still valid, without first going to the source.

Assur and his proposal team brought together all the elements of the proposal into a bound document. He had previously made an appointment to meet with Chireford to, as he put it, "turn interest into conviction for tackling this personnel/sales issue." Assur and the senior marketing person from At Ease, Inc., drove to the Puritan Agency. Arriving early for the appointment, they walked around the grounds. Joe commented that the "gift" of the unsolicited proposal should help build upon the rapport established at the first meeting.

Mary Chireford was warm and cordial to both men. As they sat around a small glass-topped table facing the picturesque rolling hills, Joe began:

JA: We took our last conversation to heart and mind, and we have come up with a response to your concerns.

MC: Oh?

JA: This proposal consists of two approaches, each of equal value, to address the issue at hand. The final choice is your decision.

MC: Interesting. Haven't heard of this dual-approach technique before.

JA: All of our proposals are tailor made. We won't make a suit that doesn't "fit."

MC: You know, Joe, this proposal you've presented is to help take care of our employee/new customer dilemma. Strange—I had wondered what happened to your firm . . .

JA: Had happened to our firm?

MC: Yes, closing date on responses to our concern was a week ago. Didn't you ask for a copy of the solicitation I generated for consulting services?

JA: No, we did not.

MC: Hmmm, according to Puritan's regulations, no consulting work can be done without competitive bidding, so, of course, we had to bring in a few proposals before any contract could be awarded.

JA: The oversight is unfortunate. However, since you have not made a decision yet, could you put our effort into your decision "hopper"?

MC: Even if I could, Joe, I see that under your cost proposal you have broken up the method of payment into three equal amounts: beginning, midway, and at the end of the contract. Again, we don't work that way. Billing is to be done monthly after progress report approval, and checks are made out subsequently. It appears you forgot some key information.

JA: Well, I'm sorry to hear that what seemed to have been a small oversight on our part was instead a major error. Next time we'll know better.

A follow-up debriefing between Assur and his staff showed a lack of strategy in fitting the proposal concept into the procurement process of the Puritan Agency.

SPECIAL TOPIC: HOW WELL CAN CLIENT AND CONSULTANT BE MATCHED?

One factor that serves to catalyze the working relationship between consultant and client is the professional and personal compatibility of both people. The client is operating in the goal-oriented environment of an organization whose existence is based on the repetition of certain tasks. Consultants are called in to work with the client to create a satisfying environment in which these goals will continue to be met. The professional camaraderie of a close working relationship is often necessary to accomplish their mutual tasks. How then, does the client know that he will be able to establish this type of working relationship—by instinct, intuition, or insight?

When the client is carrying out his other responsibilities within the organization while attempting to procure consulting services, there is not much time to determine which prospective consultant is the best one. The compatibility viewpoint gets "shoved under the rug" more times than not, often resulting in an incompatible match between consultant and client. Should the client employ a consultant whose job it is to screen and place complementary consultants according to the client's specifications?

This is obviously not a realistic solution, since consultants are not used every day, at least not in most client establishments. Also, pinpointing a compatible peer is difficult because the factors that determine compatibility are vague and subject to change. And, even if such a match could be made, how could its permanence be measured? Some recent theory and experiments that might improve the client's ability to select a compatible consultant have grown out of the difficulty of measuring such perceptual differences.

Carl C. Jung (1923) was one of the first individuals to note that people perceive information in two ways: either through sensations, focusing their attention on details of the data itself, or through intuition, focusing their attention on relationships between data items. The two ways are generally mutually exclusive. He also noted that people make decisions either by the use of rational thought and analytical means of reasoning, or by the use of value judgments and reliance on instinct. These two ways are generally also mutually exclusive. Since most client-managers collect and evaluate data to make decisions, it is helpful to understand the way in which they perceive the world (Mintzberg 1971).

By selecting one data dimension and one decision dimension, we can form four unique pairs of personality types:

1. Sensation-thinking
2. Sensation-feeling
3. Intuition-thinking
4. Intuition-feeling

It has been hypothesized that these four personality types will have differing perceptions of their organizations and will tend to define and resolve issues in different ways (Leifer 1978). A test has been developed that bears out this hypothesis (Briggs 1976). The findings imply that clients should become more aware of what "type" they are so that they can pose questions to determine if the client and consultant are compatible in the ways they perceive information and make decisions. It also means that the consultant can explore the compatibility factor by presenting his view of the data analysis and decision-making functions to the client and evaluating the client feedback. This activity would not occur in isolation from the other steps of the consultant selection process. An effort to achieve compatibility of styles implies that in the struggle for defining, resolving and implementing changes within the organization, the consultant and client will move toward a *common* process and perspective of change.

RESULTS OF THE MEETING:
CLIENT BARRIERS AND CONCERNS

What has the consultant been able to discern about the client's needs that would restrict the assignment? Answering this question requires an understanding of the explicit and implicit concerns which the client has or is likely to have. Some of these concerns which could emerge in the first session are

- The desire to be heard and to understand quickly and clearly what the consultant is saying;
- The need to know the time frame of activities and to be sure of their priority;
- The ability to retain authority and responsibility for the assignment;
- The recognition of certain inbred resistances to the changes likely to emerge through resolving the issue;
- The use of independent, patient, and secure thinking by both parties in resolving the issue;
- The sensitivity to work well with the consultant to resolve any frictions that may arise (G. Lippett 1969; Schwartz 1958; Mial 1959).

The responsibilities of client and consultant require an open-minded attitude and a willingness to work toward more satisfying situations. But, the willingness must be reaffirmed as conditions change throughout the consulting process. The client may air concerns about the maintenance of authority, the threat of an outsider, potential conflicts in the definitions of various people's involvement, the need for quick solutions, and the inability to understand the real issue. The consultant must foster, through the "responsible attitude" described in box 3.1, a supportive environment in which these concerns can be examined. If the "how" instead of the "why" of the issue is pursued, these concerns can be addressed in a spirit of mutual inquiry that will preclude their becoming negative factors in the client-consultant relationship.

REVIEW AND EXTENSION

In securing a consulting contract, a client acknowledges that he has a concern requiring assistance external to the immediate client staff. A proposed work effort is written, consultants are contacted, proposals are received, and a contract is normally let to a winner. The background, motivations, and interactions of client and consultant are all factors in stimulating a better proposal process and potential client-consultant relationship.

From the client's first recognition of the need for consulting services to the contract award, the interpersonal, interactive nature of procurement has been stressed in this chapter. The client takes the initiative in instigating meetings, conducting searches for competent proposers, and judging the merits of the proposals. During this stage, the consultant is the astute observer. By getting a glimpse of the client environment, researching the organization's activities, and perceptively responding to the request for contract work, the consultant can leave a favorable impression with the client that could set the tone for their relationship throughout the consulting assignment. In case example 4.2, the consultant made some basic, simple errors which foreclosed the opportunity to make further impressions.

Thus, both parties are responsible for exerting high-quality efforts to understand their compatibility in terms of personal style and working philosophies. This can be done by exploring perceptual differences. As case example 4.1 points out, the entry motif can also be a significant catalyst for establishing and building rapport. The next chapter builds upon this foundation of trust as the basis for the rest of the engagement.

From the contract clarification activity, the consultant can derive a clearer understanding of the client's motivation for securing his services and some clues about the client's attitude toward the consultant, the project, and the results. This understanding is deepened by the access granted to the consultant to collect information through public documents, internal files, observation, and interviews with members of the client group. (More is said on data gathering in chapter 6.) This client-consultant exchange shows the consultant what the client's stance is toward interaction and the likelihood of any change in the client's attitudes.

The second goal of the meeting is for the client, consultant, and their respective staffs to meet and become more familiar with the project. Mutual tours of client and consultant facilities can be arranged. In this way, the client gains a broader view of the consultant's situation, and the consultant's impressions are validated by the opinions and observations of the other consulting team members. This stage of the process brings the consulting assignment into clearer focus for all interactors.

After this meeting, the consultant group normally has a debriefing session to share their impressions of the client's stated and unspoken concerns. One assessment technique that can be used in the debriefing session is for each member of the group to write up his opinion of the meeting, including his perception of how the team felt about itself and about the other group. Next, these notes are shared with the group. The tone of the notes can be critical, as long as they do not close the door to further dialogue. This is also an excellent way to foresee any obstacles that may arise in developing the client-consultant relationship.

Chapter 5

Beginning the Engagement

OVERVIEW

This chapter deals with the part of the consulting process known as Engagement Beginning. At this stage, the consultant and client meet again to verify the scope of the work, identify client resources available to the consultant, and work out any logistical problems. Not only are the specifics of the consulting assignment reaffirmed, but basic communication patterns are developed between client and consultant as well. Strategies for change and a deeper understanding of client concerns and priorities also emerge that will be useful throughout the entire consulting process.

ASSUMPTIONS AND FURTHER OBSERVATIONS

In quickly scanning the past four chapters, the basic assumptions of the client and consultant working relationship are again brought to light. Once the client has decided to search for consulting assistance, he contacts various consultants, scrutinizes their abilities, judges their proposals, and formulates impressions of compatibility. From these actions, the present consultant is selected. Likewise, the consultant has decided to compete for the assignment, has responded with his best efforts in the oral discussion and written submittal, and has concluded that an effective relationship could be established with the client. Both client and consultant have implicitly agreed to carry out their respective responsibilities in an atmosphere of mutual support and cooperation.

Now that the champagne glasses have stopped clinking, the consultant meets with the client to accomplish two goals. The first is to reaffirm a mutual commitment to the consulting effort. The contract is reviewed to verify the understandings of each party to the agreement. If the client or consultant wishes to make any minor changes, and if the changes are within the scope of the contractual regulations, they are usually incorporated into the agreement at this time. If difficulties arise, informal negotiations occur to reach agreement on all points.

SPECIAL TOPIC: THE CONSULTATION SETTING

The physical setting in which consulting occurs is seldom considered as a variable which influences the performance of the consulting process, but the nature of the surroundings can indeed make a difference. There are three aspects of a setting:

1. Physical properties. Factors such as the size of a conference table, the amount of noise, the degree of illumination, ventilation, or the room temperature affect the *kinds of activity* that occur there.
2. Descriptive properties. Whether or not food is allowed, whether the door is open or closed, or whether people will be speaking directly or through tele-conferencing are all examples of variables that define the *attitude* of the setting.
3. Behavioral properties. Ways of interacting in a place or feelings about a particular place define the *expectations* about the activity (Steele 1975; Schein 1969).

The setting can positively influence the consulting engagement by

- Stimulating interaction between consultant and client,
- Being a catalyst for observing different behavior patterns, and
- Enabling the consultant to "test" organizational changes.

As with appearance, the physical properties of the setting are more important at the beginning of an assignment than toward the end. The setting should elicit a neutral or positive initial reaction and help put the consultant and client at ease. If the descriptive or behavioral properties of the environment create undue stress in either person, consideration should be given to changing the location. The setting establishes the tone for the interaction of client and consultant.

As the consultant becomes aware of the client situation and understands how the client and client group are interacting with their organizational setting, a change of locale could provide added insight into the behaviors of the client and client group. The consultant has been observing the group on their "home ground," trying to understand the situations and causes of the issue. The client group may behave differently in unfamiliar surroundings, such as a nearby hotel or conference center. A less structured atmosphere will often encourage more complete and honest appraisals of the issue and its likely resolutions from the client group.

Once a course of action is agreed upon, it may be advantageous to examine the necessary changes and their applications away from the work environment, in order to generate client reaction and feedback. The neutral setting allows the client group to consider new patterns of work activity with an open-minded attitude, untainted by the myopic perspective of the workplace and away from possible pressure by others in the organization.

The off-site interaction also enables the client and client group to focus on the proposed changes' longer-term ramifications on the goals of the organization. A change of setting, effectively used, will foster a willingness on the part of the client to examine new solutions to old problems with a fresh eye.

FACILITATING CLIENT RESPONSIVENESS TO CHANGE

The effective use of appropriate strategies can foster a client attitude that is amenable to organizational changes. A strategy is a communications device which the consultant uses to enhance and expand the client-consultant interaction. A role, in contrast, confines the relationship between the two by limiting the emphasis and effort given to an assignment by the consultant. A strategy reinforces the desire and commitment to change as the consulting process proceeds. A consultant selects and uses a strategy or strategies in response to the client's behavior (French 1978; Zaltman 1977; Goodstein 1978). A strategy consists of the following characteristics:

1. Type of communication. What communication attitude should the consultant take? There are four possibilities (as described in more detail later): a passive-empathetic mode of relating to the client, a passive-rational mode, an active-rational mode, and an active-empathetic mode. For all modes, the consultant must listen closely to the client; respond when appropriate in clear, understandable terms; and try to take a positive view of the situation (Koehler 1976; Andreychuck 1964).
2. Degree of control. This characteristic determines how the consultant will carry out the strategy. It is a function of how much the

consultant feels the interaction with the client needs to be directed and how much the client can or should lead. There are three degrees of control: total control, shared control, and no control. For consultations in which there is an emphasis on a mutually trusting relationship, the degree of control will usually vacillate between larger and smaller amounts of shared control.

3. Precipitating factor. This characteristic reveals the element of the client's situation that requires attention. It could be, for example, a particular resistance to change, a conflict with other persons in the organization, or a need for information or its clarification. In any case, the consultant's perception of the precipitating factor is usually the primary cause for choosing a strategy.

A consultant uses one or more strategies implicitly in his interaction with the client. The purpose of presenting various strategies here is to illustrate how the client-consultant relationship can be a catalyst for change, not a hindrance.

Five commonly used strategies are listed below and in figure 5.1. Each strategy reflects the desire of the consultant to heighten the effectiveness of the consulting engagement.

1. *Acceptance.* The consultant is an empathetic-passive listener. He is open to the client, listening carefully to better understand the client's perspective. The consultant wants to learn new things about the client and so chooses this strategy. The consultant's responses acknowledge that the "message" has been received. The consultant also responds with analogies or gives examples to show the client that he understands. The client seeks out the consultant with "something on his mind," and takes most of the responsibility for explaining the situation. Yet, the consultant shares some of the control by being responsive.

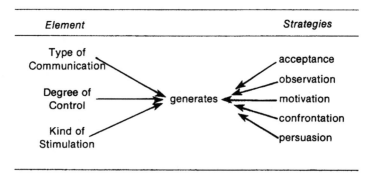

Figure 5.1.   Evolution of a Consulting Strategy

A consultant may choose this strategy for situations such as the following:

- The initial explanation of the issue
- The preliminary results of an implementation plan
- A discussion with the client's boss
- A client's personal problem

2. *Observation*. The primary thrust of this strategy is to view and record what is occurring. The consultant is a passive-rational communicator, compiling data and information about events and reporting those to the client and client group. The client retains most of the control in this strategy. The consultant exerts control only to the extent that he evaluates the information that is collected. For instance, the following assignments or phases of assignments might spur a consultant to choose this strategy:

- Collecting data on a competitor's operations
- Taking notice of how a client's machine-shop workers use their free time while at work
- Recording the performance of the implementation plan to speed up the client's cafeteria food service
- Talking with the client group to see how well prepared they were for a prior meeting with the client

3. *Motivation*. With this strategy, the consultant uses an active-rational mode in speaking with the client. The consultant has some information that he wants to convey to the client for his consideration. The former takes some control in gaining the latter's attention and making a presentation, but the client retains control over decisions stemming from it. A consultant may choose this strategy when he wishes to communicate new ideas to the client, such as the following:

- Providing a set of alternative pathways to resolving the issue
- Concisely defining the issue for the client and client group
- Demonstrating how well the issue is being resolved
- Presenting a scheme for possible future work

4. *Confrontation*. This strategy is used when conditions necessitate an encounter between the client and consultant. The communication stance used by the consultant is active, yet empathetic. The normally shared control is temporarily relinquished to the consultant. This is done so that the consultant can assist the client in dealing with something that has been difficult to handle. The emphasis is on clarifying the client's understanding of the

values implicit in a particular situation, so that intelligent and informed action can be taken. A consultant may use this strategy when the client has been reluctant to face a basic component of the issue, such as the following:

- The need to implement a new organizational structure
- The decision to lay off a key manager
- The need to delegate more authority to the operating supervisors
- The need to correct some unethical practices

5. *Persuasion.* As with the preceding strategy, the consultant is an active-empathetic communicator. Yet, unlike the preceding strategy, the consultant's objective is to convince the client of the merits of a particular action. The consultant has control during the presentation, but the client retains the authority to make final decisions. The emphasis is on persuading the client to do something of mutual interest that would not have been necessary under previous or expected conditions. The following are some situations that may trigger a consultant's choice of this strategy:

- The prospective client-consultant dialogue
- The need for review of the assignment after contract termination
- The validation of data analyses by an independent source
- The increasing number of final reports required due to unexpected demand

Two other strategies, teaching and coercion, are excluded because of their unsuitability for the consulting process. The teaching strategy, in which an instructor methodically feeds ideas to a recipient, is a one-way, noninteractive form of communication. Likewise, the coercion strategy, in which the consultant completely directs the actions of the client, is also a violation of the interactive, trusting relationship required for the consulting process to succeed.

Any of the preceding five strategies, either alone or in combination, can be used to effectively respond to a problematic situation at any stage of the consulting process. The strategies are called forth to cope with the day-to-day struggle to accomplish the assignment. Knowing when and where to call forth a strategy is one of the skills that successful consultants develop with experience.

Case Example 5.1. Strategy for a Setting

"Why can't we put the new campaign drive into 20 states?" Phil Donait asked the group matter-of-factly. "If we had more time and a less-pressured environment we could probably figure out a way," one of the representatives answered. This exchange took place at the weekly meeting of Affiliated Charities and Training (ACT). ACT, Inc., is a large philanthropic organization whose mission is to generate charitable contributions. A year ago, a representative system of management was instituted in which employees from each of the departments met weekly with Phil Donait, the managing director, to discuss and manage the activities of ACT. Recently, attendance at the meetings had declined and the performance of the organization was beginning to suffer. At a meeting a few weeks ago, Phil asked for people's thoughts on how to improve the situation, and one of the suggestions was to bring in an outside consultant to "watch us in action and find out what's wrong."

Phil took the advice and called Power, Education, and People, a firm specializing in motivational problems. Liz Sizemore, the consulting group principal, met with Phil at ACT, Inc., a week later. "Let's go into the conference room where we have our weekly meeting," Phil said after some preliminary conversation. He explained the situation and asked Liz to sit in on the next few weekly meetings. Agreeing to observe the organization for a while, Liz came to the next three meetings. After the third, she met alone with Phil in the conference room to discuss her perceptions.

"It's strange, Phil. If I could turn off the audio and just have the video it would seem that everything is okay But this is not the case. My chats with representatives, plus our conversations after each session, have shown me the subtleties of the situation. First of all, the setting of these meetings is in a conference room right next to your office. The room is elegantly furnished with closed drapes, recessed lighting, shag carpeting, subdued paintings, heavy black chairs and a u-shaped table with you in the 'saddle.' Although you ask for people's ideas, they feel it is an exercise in pointlessness because you seem to disregard their recommendations when it comes time to make a final decision. For them, this room has come to represent a frustrating situation in which their input is solicited with apparent goodwill, but seldom has an impact on the matter under discussion. As a result, Phil, they simply don't feel comfortable in your conference room."

"This is one of the most comfortable meeting rooms I know of," Phil rejoined.

"But don't you see that, comfortable or not, these people feel it is a mockery for them to be representatives if they can't participate in making decisions?" Liz persisted.

"I don't know what these people want. I . . ."

"Phil, what the departmental representatives want is to be heard. They have asked on several occasions that the setting be changed to a place where people feel more at ease."

"Yes, I know. I've considered it . . ."

"Well, consider it again, this time with the intention of letting it happen."

"I don't know—I'm not sure."

"Phil, you have a fear—a fear that somehow outside of your turf you may lose control. But if you don't concede to their wishes, you're going to lose some good people, if you haven't already. My firm has a cabin about an hour's drive from here. There are hiking trails; a lake for sailing, canoeing, and swimming; rivers for fishing; and horseback riding nearby. The cost is minimal and the place is far enough from the everyday surroundings to allow people to relax and unwind. Why don't you use it for one of your meetings? Trying this is much less painful, Phil, than thinking about it."

"Big actions come in small steps," Phil conceded. "I'll give it a try."

Phil brought up the subject at the next meeting. Liz discussed her ideas with the group, and with everyone's okay, arrangements were made. Thirty days later, the weekend meeting took place. As Liz described, the weekend was a cross between a retreat and a vacation. She conducted only two sessions: one on Friday night and the other on Sunday morning. The rest of the time was free. The Friday evening session was an open-ended time for people to interact with each other, find out more about each other's interests, and discuss some ideas for working better with each other. Individuals were encouraged to spend time during the rest of the weekend with as many other people as they could comfortably. The Sunday session was for reflection and wrap up: to discuss what the participants gained from the experience, what insights they had, and how they could interact more effectively.

Problems with applying these insights and feelings were aired, and the participants were encouraged to help each other find ways to overcome them.

Overall, the weekend was a rousing success. Everyone came away with a greater sense of involvement and an increased desire for further participation. Phil had enjoyed being "one of the boys" and had realized (throughout the course of the retreat) how little real listening he had been doing. He quietly resolved to be more open to recognizing and dealing with the concerns of his colleagues. In fact, Phil now wants future meetings to operate by consensus.

Due to the success of the retreat, ACT, Inc., is thinking of conducting retreats regularly for its affiliates and other members of its own organization.

Case Example 5.2. Initiating a Strategy

Overseas Development and Consulting (OVER), Inc., is a small, United States–based consulting firm that does agricultural planning and technology transfer for developing countries. Dr. R. J. Flack had recently been hired to serve as project director for OVER's activities in Kenya. R.J. had previously held positions with the Agency for International Development, the United Nations, and the World Bank. He is an independent thinker who is used to doing things his own way. Marilyn Able, a principal of OVER, Inc., has been experiencing particular tensions with R.J. over the way the two Kenya projects should be managed. Marilyn believes that they should use as many people from the firm or the United States on the projects as possible, since the technical know-how is often superior. She thinks that local people should be hired only as a backup. R.J. believes just the opposite and is seeking to hire many people from Nairobi to work with him.

Marilyn was at an International Consulting Association meeting not long ago, and was introduced to me by a mutual colleague. My name is Sheila Accord, and I am director of training services for Washington Integrated Learning Laboratory, Inc. Over a Dubonnet, Marilyn told me of the conflict. Although I don't usually take on individual-oriented assignments, I told her I'd explore it further, because I thought I might be able to help. We settled on a meeting time and place.

Ten days later, I met with Marilyn at OVER, Inc. In preparation for this consultation, I had made a few phone calls to consultants involved in developing countries. Their consensus validated R.J.'s position that projects tend to be successful if local people are hired and used effectively. I came to the meeting ready to defend R.J.'s view. It turned out to be the wrong strategy. Marilyn said, "I don't care how he uses the personnel resources available to him as long as we can communicate about it!" From that point on I listened empathetically while Marilyn explained why she felt hostile toward R.J. From the first meeting after R.J.'s employment contract was signed, Marilyn felt he was trying to upstage her. I asked some questions and made a few responses, but mostly listened to Marilyn explain how the situation had since deteriorated and now seemed to be out of control. I replied that if control was the issue, Marilyn should assert her authority and not wait for R.J. to get off his high horse. Marilyn agreed, and we discussed possible approaches to the man and the issue. She decided to go to Kenya and straighten things out between them.

We talked for a while longer about how Marilyn could interact with R.J., what things to be aware of, and how she might handle some of his responses. Two techniques emerged that seemed most useful: repetition and strategy. With the first, I advised Marilyn to repeat to R.J. what she heard him saying and ask, "Is this what you mean?" and suggest to R.J. that he do the same with her. With the latter, I demonstrated how she could use one of the five strategies to set the communication tone and maximize the information exchange between her and R.J. We settled on the motivation strategy as the best choice, since this would allow her to affect the decisions R.J. would subsequently make in a direct and positive way, and without having to enter into "power play" with him. Marilyn flew to Kenya the following week. She called me on her return, and told me that after two days of almost nonstop meetings, she and R.J. had ironed out their differences, established a new rapport, and developed the personnel management plan for each project. Marilyn also found that the process of working through her perceptions and turning them into positive actions was a universal one that could be successfully applied elsewhere in her professional life.

These two case studies demonstrate how to apply the communication strategies described earlier in the chapter. In case example 5.1, a confrontation strategy helped create a congenial environment in which higher employee commitment was engendered. In case example 5.2, a motivation strategy allowed two clients to work through their tensions.

Proficiency with strategies is obtained through practice. However, the true test of a consultant's use of strategies is the degree to which the *client* can use them successfully to solve his own issues after the consultant intervention.

REVIEW AND EXTENSION

The poet W. H. Auden once wrote that for a person to love himself, he must create a totally different image of himself than that which others have of him. His words are a good summary of the intent of this chapter. At the start of a new endeavor, it is crucial that all involved parties establish and begin to maintain some kind of relationship. Many factors enter into the creation of rapport, including the following:

- The client and consultant sustaining their perceptions of the other
- The ability to work together
- The effect of the physical surroundings on the interactions between client and consultant
- When and how the consultant can formulate and apply strategies toward the continuation of the client-consultant relationship

Although a consulting strategy is not a role as described in chapter 3, both strategy and role are ways of making an impression. Both can convey the consultant's confidence and ability by mirroring the client's values and complementing his mannerisms. The major difference, however, is that playing a prescribed role prevents the consultant from communicating his attitudes, impressions, or values. The role acts as a mask and creates the danger that the consultant can become the role he portrays. This can be a problem because the use of a role stifles the consultant's desire to adapt to the consulting assignment and eventually prohibits him from responding effectively to the needs of the client. During the consulting process there may be times when various kinds of feedback are requested and given by both client and consultant (see chapter 7), when consultant assistance in dealing with client resistance to change or conflict is called for (see chapter 8), and when the consultant and client evaluate each other's performance as well as their own (see chapter 9). The role will keep the consultant in the same behavior pattern and possibly decrease his sensitivity to the client. A strategy approach to developing a client-consultant relationship allows the consultant to respond to changing circumstances and still be consistent with his beliefs and understandings. Such actions, in turn, sustain behavior which is true to self and permit the necessary receptivity and flexibility in carrying forth the consulting process.

Chapter 6

Defining the Issue

OVERVIEW

With this chapter, the real effort of the consulting assignment begins. The consultant is now prepared to devote all available resources to defining the issue and validating this definition. The consultant and client meet to discern the client's current understanding of the issue and the underlying factors that are creating the issue. The consultant next obtains client permission to talk with various members of the client group and organization. The purpose of these discussions is the discovery by the consultant of the issue's root causes. The consultant then verifies those causes with those mentioned by the client and client group and in the consultant proposal. A complete description of the issue is presented to the client and client group. After some discussion and possible changes to the issue definition, the client and consultant reach consensus.

Techniques and procedures are presented in the skills section for defining an issue and conducting an interview. Data-handling and data-gathering methods are also portrayed and critiqued in the body of the chapter. The outcome of this chapter, a fully defined issue, is the crucial first step in resolving that issue.

ASSUMPTIONS AND FURTHER OBSERVATIONS

In order to assess the many factors that influence and define an issue, the consultant must first understand the organizational fabric into which the

issue is woven. This awareness is gained largely by collecting and analyzing data in the organization.

However, the simple process of information gathering makes the consultant part of the very process he is studying. The additional effects of
his input are to create new data and to intervene in the organizational
process. The creation of new data is caused by the synthesis of data which
was previously unrelated. The intervention occurs through the quest for
various kinds of information. In either case, the consultant must be aware
of the possible effects of his information gathering and try to separate his
influence from the information. That is, in defining the issue, there are
five sorts of information quality:

1. The client's current perception of the issue
2. The raw, unaltered facts related to the issue
3. The raw, consultant-derived facts related to the issue
4. The opinions and qualitative assessments of the client group
5. The consultant's definition of the issue

An early acknowledgment of these multiple data types by both client
and consultant can contribute to a realistic assessment of the client's situation and issue. This assessment occurs by relating fact and opinion, and
by the frequency of response to the significance of each factor. Organizational perceptions, client perceptions, and consultant perceptions must
also be evaluated. Once the issue definition procedure is put into motion,
change begins.

SKILLS SECTION: HOW TO DEFINE AN ISSUE

There are three elements that constitute this activity: a *mode*, a *dynamic*,
and an *attitude*.

The *mode* is a creative one, with four phases:

1. In the *preparation phase*, the issue is brought up to a common, current
   level of understanding.
2. An *incubation phase* follows during which the issue is deliberately
   not discussed.
3. The *insight phase* occurs when flashes of inspiration lead to a fuller
   understanding of the root causes of an issue.
4. Finally, in the *verification phase*, the arrived-at issue definition is
   measured against past experience, collected information, and others'
   ideas to sustain its validity (Raybould and Minter 1971).

The *dynamic* is a facilitative element. A picture of the dynamic would show these steps:

1. *Warm-up.* The client and client group are convened by the consultant in a neutral setting. The consultant may ask some colleagues of his to attend, perhaps one with no prior exposure to the type of issue under discussion and another who has dealt with similar issues in the past. The consultant introduces all parties and tries to set a comfortable working tone for the meeting with his opening remarks.

2. *Issue description.* The consultant explains the purpose of the session, the agenda, and the hoped-for results. The participants are asked for their written response to questions (box 6.1) that the consultant has prepared in advance. Sufficient time is allotted for everyone to give complete and thoughtful answers.

3. *Issue viewpoint.* The consultant now shares with the group his information and insight about the issue. This is augmented and clarified by the members in a free-wheeling exchange. The two outside participants can also interject comments as they see fit. By the end of the first part of the session, the consultant will have written down the group sense of the nature of the issue. This issue statement should not be couched as an implied solution, a dilemma, or a vague problem. Rather, the statement should define the issue in specific, operational terms and relate it directly to those most involved (Elbing 1978).

4. *Gestation.* This period is the break between the two parts of the session (usually overnight) in which the ideas and perceptions are given time to settle in each participant's mind. New relationships or perspectives may also emerge during this stage.

5. *Restatement of issue.* The group and the consultant meet once more to collect and share additional input. The consultant gives the members a second questionnaire, which attempts to bring the causes of the

---

Box 6.1. Defining the Issue

1. What is the issue?
2. How did it originate?
3. What has been done about the issue to date?
4. What do you think are the causes of the issue?
5. In one sentence, what is the issue?
6. What do you see as your input to the issue situation at this point?
7. What objective do you hope to accomplish as a result of taking action on the issue?

Box 6.2.   Identifying Issue Causes

1. Choose a topic which you know well and like, but which is unrelated to the client issue area (CIA). State the topic.
2. Can an issue be found in this topic which resembles the CIA? Describe this topic issue (TI).
3. What similar characteristics are there between the two issues?
4. What are the differences between the CIA and TI?
5. What are the causes of the TI?
6. Does your answer to the previous question suggest new causes of the CIA?
7. Did the use of a comparative issue deepen your understanding of the CIA? If so, how? If not, why not? If not, can you find a more useful comparison?

issue into sharper focus (box 6.2). The consultant keeps track of the key elements that arise from the discussion.

6. *Consensus.* An open discussion follows, until a consensus is reached on all issue causes. The consultant asks that each person sign the two questionnaires and collects them for future reference.

The *attitude* throughout the process should be nonjudgmental. The participants should be encouraged not to criticize the ideas put forth, but to offer clarifying statements.

All ideas should be accepted as of equal worth and explored impartially. The questions that are asked should require thoughtful, unprejudiced answers and encourage the participants to build on the ideas of others.

Thus, defining an issue can be done through open collaboration with no hidden agendas. If an atmosphere of confidence and trust is established at the outset, the issue can be examined objectively without any preconceived bias or imposition of predetermined group attitudes (Gibb 1961).

HOW TO CONDUCT AN INTERVIEW

The purpose of an interview is to obtain some desired information. A close look at the components of an interview will help demystify what is, for many, a cryptic procedure. The following elements are necessary for a successful interview:

- The interviewer must be well trained in the art and technique of interviewing.
- There must be a depth of commitment on the part of both interviewer and respondent.

- There must be sufficient time allotted for the interview.
- There must be productive preparation for the interview (McGill 1977).

Throughout the consulting process, there is a constant need for working with information. The interview is one basic method of accessing information. Table 6.1 shows the role of interviewing at each stage in the consulting process. There is no interviewing in the Issue Recognition stage as client-consultant contact has not yet been made. The Monitoring and Termination stage has the consultant writing up the consulting assignment and little, if any, additional information is requested. For the purpose of this discussion, the interview will be limited to the specific information requirements stemming from the definition of the issue. There are four basic types of interviews: the mailed interview, the telephone interview, the online interview, and the face-to-face interview. These are described in table 6.2 and can be used singly or in combination, depending upon the specific situation. The sought-after information can be anything from specific detailed data to general, conceptual impressions.

No matter what the purpose or nature of the interview, the following common elements are necessary for its success:

1. *Definition of the purpose of the interview.* Knowing the client definition of the issue, the consultant prepares to obtain information either to substantiate the hypothesized causes of the issue, to validate alternatives for resolving the issue, to evaluate the implementation of resolution pathways, or to monitor the longer-term viability of the resolved issue in the client's organizational environment.

2. *Identification of the objectives of the interview.* The consultant outlines the specific kinds of information needed from the respondent. He measures the proposed scope against client expectations to ensure that it is not too broadly directed or too narrowly focused. The outcome of the interview is specified.

3. *Translation of the objectives into a question format.* The consultant asks questions that he thinks are likely to reveal the required information. The first question should be interesting and engaging, and should help the respondent to feel at ease. Subsequent questions should build up the respondent's confidence, so that he can answer more subtle and sensitive questions. The list of questions is a guide to exploring the client's territory and should not restrain discussion from related topics. The guide is edited and tested and usually forwarded to the respondents prior to the interview.

4. *Selection of the order of interviews and respondents.* The consultant decides what series, if any, of interviews is necessary, whom to interview, and in what order. Any pertinent qualifications of respondents are obtained. (Note: the people to be interviewed can be part of the client

Table 6.1. Interviews in the Consulting Process

Stage	Interviewer	Interviewee	Objective	Frequency
Issue Recognition	Client[a]	—	Client discerns need for consulting	—
Consultant Selection	Client[a]	Consultant[a]	Client chooses consultant	Once or twice on different days
Engagement Beginning	Consultant	Client	Consultant clarifies scope of work	Once
Issue Definition	Consultant	Client and/or other[b]	Consultant unearths causes of issue	Multiple times, multiple days (usually one per person)
Resolution Pathways	Consultant	Client	Consultant finds means to resolve issue	Multiple times, multiple days
Pathway Implementation	Consultant	Client	Consultant develops plan for resolution	Once
Monitoring and Termination	—	—	Consultant verifies plan and writes final report	—
Evaluation and Follow-Up	Client	Consultant	Client requests additional services	Multiple times, multiple days

[a] "Consultant" refers to the primary consultant and consultant group. "Client" refers to the primary client group.
[b] "Other" refers to either people in the organization outside the client group or any relevant contacts in other organizations.

Table 6.2. Types of Interviews

Type	Description	Advantages	Disadvantages
Mailed	Brief, factual answers Six- to eight-week lead time	Means of reaching large and/or widely scattered group	Is impersonal and prohibits interpretative questions
	Usually with middle management	Allows respondent time to formulate answers	Has low response rate Requires lengthy response time Requires lengthy preparation time
Telephone	Brief, factual answers	Efficient means of reaching a large number of people	Limits extended discussions
	Five- to seven-day lead time	Useful for quickly updating information	Is impersonal and eliminates possibility of nonverbal cues
	Usually with middle management		Prohibits use of visual material
Face-to-Face	Factual or conceptual answers	Interactive process to observe and motivate respondent	Difficult to arrange in terms of mutual availability and mutual location
	Five- to seven-day lead time	On-the-spot explanation and interpretation of both questions and answers	Tendency of respondent to "put on an act" and answer deceptively
	Usually with top management or middle management Also used with employees	Gains current information from key people	
On Line	Brief, factual answers Two- to four-week lead time Usually with middle management Also used with employees	Means of reaching large and/or widely scattered group Allows respondent to formulate answers immediately	Is impersonal and prohibits interpretative questions Not usually scheduled ahead of time

group, part of the larger organization, or outside the organization, depending upon the purpose of the interview.)

5. *Establishment of the initial interview contact with respondents.* The consultant generally makes arrangements for the interview(s) ahead of time. Working through proper organizational channels, the prospective

interviewees are given written notice that outlines the purpose of the meeting and suggests a time and place for the interview. If the interview is to be
face-to-face, a setting is chosen that is quiet, free from interruptions, conve-
nient, and comfortable for the respondent. Date and place arrangements are
discussed and agreed to by both parties shortly before the face-to-face or
telephone interview.

6. *Conduct of the interview.* For the mailed or online interview, the respondent simply answers the questions and returns the completed interview to the consultant. For the telephone or face-to-face interview, an
interactive mode is used to motivate the respondent and sustain interest
throughout. The consultant prefaces the interview with a brief explanation of why it is being conducted and how the information will be used.
The time required, the expectations of the respondent, and the confidentiality of the acquired information are discussed. The consultant should
also supply some professional background information on himself. Using
the list of questions as a guide, the consultant proceeds with the interview. The atmosphere for dialogue should be informal and open, yet
directed toward certain kinds of information.

The consultant wants to obtain clear, complete answers without
conducting an interrogation. He can accomplish this by listening to the
answer, recording it, and asking some probing questions to clarify it.
The probing can be done directly by asking a straightforward question,
or indirectly by using various listening responses effectively. One useful
technique is for the interviewer to rephrase an answer from the respondent, and ask if his understanding is correct. In this way, both parties
move toward a more complete mutual understanding. A nonjudgmental attitude can be conveyed by the effective use of these exploratory
techniques.

7. *Conclusion of the interview.* Keeping closely to the time allotted, the
consultant either asks for more time if the interview is going well or
is incomplete, or wraps up the questioning. The questions are quickly
reviewed and the respondent's answers are summarized. This ensures
response accuracy, and allows the respondent to look objectively at his
answers, modifying them as appropriate. The consultant arranges for a
telephone or additional face-to-face interview if it is required and may ask
the respondent for additional leads or sources.

8. *Evaluation of the interview.* The interview information is reviewed and
notes are taken as soon as possible after the interview. The factual data
should be scrutinized for relevancy to the issue. Opinions and interpretation of the respondent and the interviewer should be included in the written evaluation. All other consultant team members should receive copies,
which will form the basis for discussion sessions with the client, progress
reports, and input to the next step of the consulting process.

When the interviewing is being done by a group of consultants, each consultant or consultant team should conduct a test interview. Then, all consultants should meet and discuss these test interviews and make modifications as needed. The rest of the interviews should be uniformly conducted, based on the test results. When there is a small number of telephone or face-to-face interviews, another possible variation is to mail the questionnaires and solicit answers prior to the actual interview. In this situation, the interview becomes a time to *collect* and *evaluate* the responses (Kubr 1976; Downs 1977; Metzler 1977).

DIAGNOSIS OF THE ISSUE

Using the issue definition means described in the skills section, the consultant gathers information about the issue and its underlying symptoms. With this data, the consultant completes the following steps to substantiate and fully explicate the issue:

A. Writes a concise paragraph about the client issue. This includes its definition, its causes, and any supporting evidence.
B. Relates the issue to the larger organizational context by considering its relationship to
1. The goal and objectives of the organization and client group,
2. The long-range organization action plan, and
3. Other relevant organizational programs or procedures.
C. Interprets the stated issue causes to determine whether they are actually causes or symptoms, based on his acquired knowledge of
1. The past history of client operations, and
2. The organization and client group structure, functions, and communication patterns.
D. Identifies personal characteristics within the client organization that are likely to have contributed to the issue.
E. Describes technical data which validate the issue causes (Seney 1963).

ISSUE DEFINITION IN THE PUBLIC SECTOR

The major difference between issue definition in the public and private sectors is the consultant's input to the description of the issue. In the private sector, the issue is first defined by the client and is subject to modification as the consultant begins the engagement. In the public sector, the consultant usually begins with the government's issue definition and then responds with a proposal that accepts that definition and proposes a resolution. The public sector client should already define his needs based on the policy and goals of his organization. The funding availability and payment scheme for the "need" have been determined and a solicitation for consulting services has been generated, based on the client definition of the issue. There is some technical clarification that can occur after the contract award, but generally few if any major changes are made to a clear issue definition in the public sector. There is only one situation in which the consultant would have direct input into the issue definition: when he is under contract for this specific purpose. This contracted task would then prohibit the consultant from bidding on the request, that is, from trying to resolve the issue (Sommers 1973).

DATA GATHERING

The functions of data gathering in the consulting process are

- To find supporting evidence for the perceptions of the issue,
- To discover new information which could lead to new insights about the issue, and
- To create a familiarity with the client's technical and behavioral situations which will allow for greater ease in implementing resolutions to the issue.

There are four fundamental ways of collecting data: observation, perusal of written records, interviews, and surveys (G. Lippett 1978; McGill 1977). The use of any of these methods depends upon the scope of consulting assistance being given. In most cases, all four methods are used to varying degrees. Some consulting assignments are oriented almost exclusively to gathering facts and opinions, for which surveys are most appropriate. Other assignments are oriented to modifying established procedures, in which case observation is the most useful method.

Determining the underlying reasons for the issue's existence also involves defining methods and intensities of data gathering. That is, the time and cost of collecting and analyzing information needs to be specified beforehand to avoid exceeding the time or cost allocations.

Briefly, the four methods involve the following:

1. Collecting information by *direct observation* implies close examination of client operations and procedures as they normally occur. Data is compiled on day-to-day activities. Tasks and behavior categories are drawn and client activities are classified into these categories. Time-motion studies (described in chapter 2) are an example of this method. The drawbacks of the direct observation method include the potential disruption of client

activities by consultant observers. The presence of the consultant may make the client group members feel self-conscious or uncomfortable, or cause them to change their normal behavior. Another limitation is the inability of this method to fully capture information on ideas or feelings, which are often only communicated indirectly.

Depending upon the situation, these drawbacks could be serious enough to jeopardize the accuracy of the information collected by this method.

2. *Examining written documents* is a primary means of formulating a current picture of the issue situation. This picture could be based on historic information, outside reports, supporting books or articles, or quantitative analyses and projections. The possible drawbacks to this method are the speed at which this information can be accessed, the amount of relevant and accurate data available, and the possible negative effects of requesting sensitive data, even if authorized.

3. *Interviews* are explained earlier in the skills section of this chapter.

4. The most common form of gaining up-to-the-minute information in an anonymous or indirect manner is the *survey*. A survey is usually a set of questions calling for a response over a range of fixed choices. The same survey is sent or given to all members of the selected group. The responses are highly amenable to statistical analyses. Many respondents can be sought out using this method and little time is required (in general) to answer all the questions. Box 6.3 provides some guidelines for constructing a survey (Walsh 1973).

The unique advantage of surveys is the low cost and short time period necessary to distribute them and compile their results. The main drawback is the inability of this method to elicit qualitative responses and the nuances of attitudes and opinions of the respondents.

No matter which methods are used to assess information, success in obtaining the necessary facts, statistics, and opinions depends upon understanding the nature of the data.

This understanding develops through careful planning which consists of determining the following characteristics of the data:

- The standard meaning of terms in the organization. For instance, knowing that the category "part-time employees" includes summer interns, temporary secretarial support, and 20-hour-per-week administrators in this client's organization could prevent accounting errors.
- The kinds of data, along with units and accuracy limits if necessary. This implies, for example, listing the energy usage of the five different boilers in common units, along with the likely margin of measurement error.
- The time period of the data need. Is the data needed for three years or six months?

- The extent of coverage of the data request. Is it necessary to obtain continuous daily information for the last five years or will monthly totals for the last three years suffice? Are individual labor wage rates required for all categories or will a sample category plus total do? Is data before a certain time relevant to current operations? Should data be collected during periods of exceptional events (strikes, layoffs, energy shortages, etc.)?
- The accessibility of the information. Are records in a format where the requested information can be easily retrieved? Are there security considerations with some of the data? Can the data be obtained with a minimum of client staff disruption?
- The end use of the data. How should the data be organized and presented? What sequence should the information follow (Baird 1978)?

Box 6.3. Guidelines for Survey Formulation

1. Explain briefly the purpose of the survey and the benefits to the respondents.
2. Decide what information is needed, based on the purpose of the survey: for example, facts about the respondent, facts about people or events known to the respondent, or the respondent's opinions.
3. Choose the basic format of the survey based on the subject matter, the respondents, and the type of analysis intended. Keep the survey questionnaire as brief as possible.
4. Determine the best sequence of questions.
5. Eliminate questions that are ambiguous or redundant.
6. Determine whether the questions permit alternative answers.
7. Determine whether the answers cover alternatives in a logical order without overlapping.
8. Test the questionnaire to discover if the form of the responses is acceptable.
9. Eliminate "leading" questions in which the answers are influenced by preceding questions.
10. Determine whether the questions are asking for information that the respondent can reasonably be assumed to possess.
11. Test the questionnaire to discover if the information sought will be provided by the respondent's answers.
12. Obtain evaluations of the first draft of the survey from different sources, and incorporate any suggested changes that will improve the questionnaire.
13. Determine whether the final editing of the survey questionnaire includes all necessary changes to its form and content so that respondents will know what they are supposed to do and why they are doing it.

Table 6.3.   Data-Gathering Techniques

Task	Techniques
Client perception of issue	Consultant note taking
Issue related to larger organizational context	Examining written documents
Causes versus symptoms	Written documents/face-to-face interview
Personal influences	Face-to-face interview/informal discussion
Technical data inputs	Written documents/survey

All these factors should be considered before data-gathering begins. This not only saves time, but also helps to focus the data search on information that is most relevant to the issue (Garvin and Bermont 1980). Thus, to fully seek out the causes of the issue, various data-gathering techniques would be used (see table 6.3).

Careful execution of the above tasks results in the identification of the real causes of the issue. After discussion with the consultant team, a presentation is prepared for the client and client group. A visual summary of the consultant's effort is found in table 6.4. It illustrates how the original understanding of the issue has been augmented by consultant examination of issue causes. The client's statements about the issue causes have been examined and have either been found to be true, false, or a symptom rather than a cause.

Reasons and data citations are offered to support this finding. Also, newly found causes are given with their reasons and citations. Together, this information serves as the basis for the updated issue definition. Comments are solicited from the client and client group. When consensus has

Table 6.4.   Causes of the Client Issue

Updated Issue Definition:

Originally Stated Cause(s):	Current Status[a]/Reasons:	Source:
a.	a.	a.
b.	b.	b.
c.	c.	c.
Newly Found Cause(s):	*Evidence/Reasons:*	*Source:*
1.	1.	1.
2.	2.	2.
3.	3.	3.

[a]Either *symptom, cause,* or *invalid.*

been reached, the consultant states his intention to pursue alternative means for resolving the defined issue.

Case Example 6.1. Can First Class Be Nth Rate?

Hay T. Evens, one of the South's oldest firms, was discreetly soliciting private bids from a few select public relations consulting firms to improve worker morale. Over the last five years there had been a slow but steady decline in management-worker relations, with productivity rates decreasing markedly. After a careful and thorough evaluation of formal proposals to rectify the morale situation, the prestigious firm of Winston Stately, Esq., was selected. Mr. Hendrick Livingston, Stately's representative, met with Mr. Randolph Barclay, vice president in charge of corporate affairs. Over midmorning coffee in Wedgewood cups, Mr. Barclay intoned, "Our present worker morale is at low ebb, I'm afraid. We at Hay T. Evens are in need of some effective inducements to increase worker performance."

Mr. Livingston returned to Stately, Esq., and created a seminar on defining and using morale boosters. The seminar included a slide presentation that dealt with morale: its origin, its likely causes of decay, and ways in which it can be strengthened to increase the bond of trust between employer and employee. Various techniques were shown to accomplish this latter course. The main purpose of the seminar was to stimulate and motivate corporate people to consider ways of improving their interaction with employees.

The one-day gathering was held away from familiar surroundings and was attended by top management, public relations and personnel staff, and employee representatives from other departments. A lot of discussion and suggestions were engendered by the morning presentation. The employee representatives in particular made several strong comments emphasizing the importance of consistency in corporate policy and behavior.

With the management of Hay T. Evens now sufficiently concerned over the state of worker morale, Livingston and Barclay met to consider the next steps. "What is our real problem?" Barclay asked. "What do you think it is?"

Livingston replied, "I'm not sure."

"I feel as if James Evens, our president, has organization anemia. His family has been the blue blood of this company for too long. I feel it is time for a change," Barclay confessed.

"Are you saying that the helmsman, Evens, is the cause of the worker malaise?" Livingston questioned.

"Yes," Barclay answered. Livingston agreed to verify Barclay's hypothesis and report back to him.

The following week, Livingston found all the newspaper stories on Hay T. Evens over the previous three years. The story lines were all similar: corporate officer meetings, stock values, and profit and loss information. After securing Barclay's permission, Livingston next interviewed staff members, individually or in small groups, from almost all the departments. The sentiment was surprisingly consistent: a dislike for management and the feeling that it was aloof, insensitive, and not open to innovation. Livingston spoke with the personnel director about the employee sentiment.

"People have been saying these things for years," the director agreed, "but nothing seems to change."

Livingston was baffled. It all seemed too easy. Employee disgruntlement with the management, management wishing to improve employee morale, and both bemoaning the other. Barclay and he were to have their weekly lunch at 1:00 p.m. that Thursday. Livingston came a bit early and stopped by the personnel department to get some information on labor contracts. "We have a progressive system at Hay T. Evens," the personnel director began. "There are no contracts, no agreements, no separate benefits or fringe packages. Instead, every employee is given a rating upon entering the company. This rating becomes a multiplier for increasing his or her share of corporate resources and profits. This system means that most employees earn more, save more, and have more choice than their counterparts elsewhere."

Over lunch with Barclay, Livingston raised the "multiplier" scheme and remarked that he thought it was a cause of employee apathy. "The incentive works well in the short term. But in the longer term, it no longer has the same positive effects." Barclay sat back in his chair and said that the system had been around as long as the company. He went on to say that if workers got out of line the multiplier could be decreased or dropped altogether, but "most people like it, so why buck it?"

Livingston wrote up his findings and recommendations to date and shared them with Evens's top management two weeks later. "It is clear," Livingston summarized, "that an effective morale-building program must influence management and labor in similar ways. It must enhance the achievement of the company goals. If nothing is done to boost morale, productivity rates can be expected to continue their decline." Two days later Hay T. Evens experienced its first work slowdown.

This case example demonstrates that to find a viable means of resolving a client issue, the consultant must go far beyond mere collection of data. In fact, as the story shows, once the morale problem was acknowledged, the issue became a question of when the company was going to take steps to correct the situation. The lesson which emerges from the case example is this: joint recognition and understanding of the issue are only half the process. Without corresponding action to resolve the issue, agreement and understanding alone will accomplish little.

REVIEW AND EXTENSION

In this portion of the consulting process, the rudiments of issue definition and data collection have been presented. A skills section of methods and techniques dealt with the issue and its underlying causes and detailed the process for conducting an interview. These consulting tools were then used to discover the root causes of the issue. The likely causes were discussed by the client and consultant in order to reach agreement about the issue.

The kinds of data, way(s) of obtaining it, its uses, and resulting effects on the understanding of the issue vary with the issue and the consultant-client interaction. The following pointers are provided to improve the data-gathering and data-analysis functions of consulting to achieve connections between issue definition and resolution:

- Data gathering requires multiple inputs. No single collection method can provide a thorough picture of the issue. This fact implies that the consultant must get to know the client, client group, client organization, and resource people to collect information. It also means that a working rapport should be attempted with all data holders in order to minimize any perceived threats to their position, abilities, potential for promotion, and so forth.
- The data needs are continuous. The organizational situation changes from consultant entry to consultant termination, and revised or new data will be required to carry out all the steps of the consulting process.
- The data should reflect the current situation. The information procured should not consist only of statistics or random anecdotes. The information should be cast in the vocabulary and context of the client and client group. Enumerations and examples should support the data, giving it credibility, orientation, and usefulness.
- The data should reflect the future situation and help prepare the client for the next step: finding a way to resolve the issue (Zaltman 1977; Kubr 1976).

Chapter 7

Pathways to Issue Resolution

OVERVIEW

Once the issue is defined, the consultant returns to his own turf to decide how to deal with it. The procedure for arriving at resolution alternatives is described in this chapter.

When several viable alternatives have been generated, they are presented to the client along with criteria for selection suited to the client's situation. A skills section is included which

- Details the feedback mechanism
- Explores the influence of meetings on the consulting process

SKILLS SECTION

I. How to Give and Receive Feedback

Feedback is a technique that is practiced often and labeled rarely. It is an intrinsic part of the consulting process and allows consultants to gauge the effectiveness of their actions.

Feedback is useful for staying in touch with client impressions and observations, and for eliciting suggestions for change or improvement. It is a mechanism to obtain information that is critical to the major decisions of the consulting assignment. Feedback provides signals to consultants that should alert them to any potential problems. These signals are clues that can be used to guide and modify their efforts (Merry 1977).

One way to explain the process of feedback is to explore its attributes and their opposites. Table 7.1 examines the paired attributes of feedback to demonstrate the full extent of the knowledge that consultants and clients can obtain, directly and indirectly, in their communications with each other. In terms of the consulting process, a few observations are relevant:

- Feedback is used at each stage of the consulting process. Whenever another person's advice, approval, opinion, or assistance is required, the feedback mechanism is used.
- Feedback is not a strategy. Rather, feedback can be spurred by the use of an effective strategy (as it is defined in chapter 5).
- Feedback can be solicited for any reason on any topic.
- Feedback must be sought with a positive attitude and sufficient knowledge to obtain what is needed.

In order for feedback to serve as the catalyst by which the various consulting strategies are realized, the consultant

- Acknowledges the stage of the consulting process,
- Perceives the stimulus necessitating communication with the client,
- Chooses the appropriate strategy,
- Matches feedback to the strategy, and
- Completes the communication.

Table 7.2 shows possible combinations of strategies and feedback. The consultant must use feedback to further the chosen strategy and move the client-consultant relationship toward issue resolution. For the client, the use of feedback increases his understanding of and involvement in the consulting process. However, as with many other facets of consulting, the feedback process should not be taken for granted, since a complete understanding of it can be useful in the choice and usage of the best possible strategy. In moving through any step of the consulting process, the chosen strategy is likely to change.

A switch in strategies means a change in the type of feedback given. Also, hybrid strategies can be produced from those in table 7.2, which will change the nature of the feedback associated with them. The strong correlation between feedback and the effective use of strategies is an ever-present factor that should not be overlooked.

How can feedback be used with success throughout the consulting process? There is no single answer. However, some things to keep in mind about feedback include the following:

- Client-consultant meetings are a natural time for the expression of feedback, arising either as an intrinsic part of the interaction or by

Table 7.1. Paired Dimensions of Feedback

Dimension	Explanation	Opposite Dimension	Explanation
Solicited	Receiver of feedback asks for it.	Spontaneous	Feedback is given without being solicited.
Evaluative	Giver attaches a judgment value to feedback.	Non-evaluative	Giver describes situation without passing judgment.
Directed	Feedback is oriented toward receiver explicitly.	Non-directed	Feedback is oriented toward receiver implicitly.
Personal	Feedback reflects giver's opinion or feelings.	Impersonal	Feedback does not include giver's opinion or feelings.
Group support	Receiver's group agrees with or supports feedback.	Group non-support	Receiver's group disagrees with or remains silent about feedback.
Positive	Feedback is praise or acceptance of receiver's effort or interactions.	Negative	Feedback is a critique or rejection of receiver's effort or interactions.
Here and now	Feedback refers to immediate or recent events.	There and then	Feedback refers to past events.
Verbal	Feedback is spoken.	Non-verbal	Feedback is communicated through gestures, facial expressions, or body language.
Technical	Feedback is of project concern.	Behavioral	Feedback is of interpersonal concern.
In private	Feedback is given one-on-one.	In public	Feedback is given by a group.
Oral	Feedback is given face-to-face.	Written	Feedback is given by communiqué, written evaluation, drawings, graphics, and so forth.
Client originated	Feedback is given by client or client group.	Other originated	Feedback is given by outside colleagues, other members of client's organization, or consultant.

direct request. In either case, its effectiveness can be enhanced by giving prior consideration to the kinds of responses that are likely to be sought and given, and their probable implications.

- If a particular concern has not been dealt with, a special session can be called to address this issue.
- Obtaining satisfactory feedback requires practice, mutual trust, and the ability to change the tone of the interaction to catalyze feedback.
- Feedback can be needed for any one of a number of reasons, from clarification to conflict resolution. Whatever the situation, the consulting process will not move forward without feedback, since it is a necessary component at any stage.
- Another reason that feedback is necessary throughout an assignment is to ensure that actual changes are congruent with consultant and client expectations.

There are no two situations in which the feedback will be identical, nor can feedback be ascertained in advance. To appreciate the importance

Table 7.2.   Strategy Use via Feedback

Strategy	Consultant Feedback[a]	Reason	Client Feedback[b]	Reason
Acceptance	Non-verbal Non-evaluative Oral	To reassure or explain	Solicited Verbal Oral	To understand or evoke camaraderie
Observation	Directed Here and now Verbal	To convey information	Solicited Group support Positive	To receive specific inputs
Motivation	Directed Technical In public	To present progress of assignment	Spontaneous Evaluative Written	To ascertain direction of assignment
Confrontation	Evaluative Personal In private	To work through client barrier	Here and now Non-verbal Non-directed	To overcome resistance
Persuasion	Solicited Oral Directed	To move client toward some action	Group support Evaluative Non-verbal	To consider some course of action

[a] Feedback used by the consultant for each strategy.
[b] Feedback used by the client for each strategy.

of feedback, it is necessary to consider the potentially disastrous consequences of a lack of feedback at each step in the consultation.

Feedback is the rudder of the consulting process, and it is crucial to the successful completion of an assignment.

II. Meetings and the Consulting Process

Meetings are basic to the consulting process. What is their basic function, and why are they so indispensable? Meetings are planned exchanges with a definite purpose—to clarify and further any given stage of the consulting process. Why couldn't this be done by a few people over lunch, or while playing volleyball, or while commuting to and from the office?

The characteristics that distinguish meetings from other forms of group encounter are five:

1. Focus. Discussion is targeted to specific areas of interest and limited by the meeting structure and time constraint.
2. Participation. All interested parties are able to interact together in the same place and at the same time.
3. Synergy. The give-and-take of person-to-person communication creates alternate positions which are generally not present in any individual's perceptions.
4. Conviction. The leadership and interaction generates a willingness to risk professional concerns and to use vocational skills to achieve certain expressed ends.
5. Timing. The tone of the meeting underscores the urgency of the issue, and conveys a sense of immediacy that results in a desire to do whatever is necessary to get the job done.

Consultant-client meetings are of two types:

1. A meeting to discuss concerns directly related to moving from step to step in the consulting process, such as a meeting held for the purpose of moving from the Engagement Beginning (data gathering) stage to the Issue Definition stage.
2. A dialogue between consultant and client, client team, or others to fulfill tasks undertaken in any stage of the consulting process. Such meetings might be necessary for a variety of reasons including in-house review (client or consultant), auxiliary data collection, or development of personal attributes or skills.

A meeting held during a consulting assignment can be characterized by its purpose and organization. It is a small-group discussion or workshop held to further a phase of the assignment. It is generally attended by two to ten people who usually know one another, although they may come from different status levels in the organization. There are, or should be, two or more objectives for a meeting, and they are addressed during the appropriate stage in the following sequence of the component parts of a meeting (Schindler-Rainman 1975a):

1. Perceiving the need for the meeting. The impetus to meet can come from several sources or motivations. The reasons for wanting a meeting are then evaluated to discern whether a meeting is the appropriate way to handle a given concern.
2. Decision. The pros and cons of the possible meeting are weighed, and a place and time for the meeting are chosen.
3. Selection of attendees. Those with concerns relevant to the issue are selected to attend the meeting.
4. Setting the agenda. The objectives of the meeting are decided upon, leaving enough time in the schedule for reaction and discussion.
5. Preparation.
   A. A location to hold the meeting is secured.
   B. Time and date are selected in accordance with the attendees' schedules.
   C. A meeting notice and agenda are sent to the attendees far enough in advance so that they can clear their schedules and prepare for the meeting.
   D. Other logistical concerns are taken care of.
6. The meeting. Those invited come to the specified place at the proper time and a meeting is held. The meeting is opened with an overview that focuses everyone's attention on the immediate purposes of the meeting. Reactions and expectations are voiced, and the items on the agenda are addressed and modified as appropriate. Finally, the results are garnered, and the accomplishments of the meeting are summarized and synthesized.
7. Debriefing. Generally, representatives from the meeting hold a follow-up session shortly afterward to evaluate the substance and the process of the meeting. Implications are drawn for further steps and future encounters (Ferner 1980).

Each meeting step is itself a meeting. The input to a particular step is the outcome of the prior meeting step. Likewise, the output from one step becomes input to the next.

Those in attendance at a meeting can have various functions. They include the following:

- *Arranger*—the person(s) in charge of organizing the meeting. This individual has the responsibilities of preparing for the meeting, recording the meeting, and/or distributing any subsequent transcripts.
- *Participants*—the persons who will affect or who are affected by the outcome of the meeting. These people have a direct interest in its proposed content.
- *Leader*—the person who generally convenes the meeting to obtain group input for pending decisions. The leader usually chairs and runs the meeting.
- *Neutral enhancers*—the people outside the context of the meeting who have no vested interests. They function either as observers of the dynamics of the group, facilitators of the meeting content, or presenters of pertinent information to catalyze or supplement discussion of agenda items (Doyle 1976).

The leader function is reserved for the client since he is the final decision maker. The participants and arrangers are usually members of the client group. The neutral enhancer is normally the consultant. The client's major challenge is to conduct productive meetings.

This requires a participative leadership framework in which all attendees are encouraged to share in the pre-meeting planning, the meeting decision making, and the post-meeting evaluation. If the participants and arrangers are not willing to share these responsibilities, then they should be prepared to accept the following as the status quo: "Our meetings don't look much different from the way they did in the medieval classrooms and parliaments; decisions still tend to be made by the leadership and passively accepted by the followers. Except that followers are getting bored and staying away from the meetings at which leaders announce their decisions" (Schindler-Rainman 1975a, 5). The leader should obtain feedback from the other participants to achieve the purpose of the meeting expeditiously. The members of the client group can help by searching for ways to anticipate and overcome problems with meetings. Can the client make meetings more successful? In many cases, the answer is "not without assistance."

The consultant can often foolishly be too preoccupied with the substance of the consulting assignment to consider the consequences of poor client meetings. An unsuccessful meeting is one in which the purpose has not been fulfilled and the dynamics have not been satisfying to the participants, an all-too-frequent result in client organizations. Ineffective meetings often lead to a less productive, less high-spirited, and less communicative client group. They will make the consultant's task more difficult.

Therefore, it is incumbent upon the consultant to consider the process and the quality of meetings his business, and not just the concern of the client.

How can consultant and client work together to improve the interaction and task achievement of their meetings? There are several ways in which this can be accomplished:

1. Timing. Discussing meetings during the early part of a consulting stage lays the groundwork for increased client involvement in the meeting process. An early awareness of the ways in which poor meetings impede the work in progress will result in larger client responsibility for effective meetings by the end of that stage.
2. Initiative. The client can bring up the subject of meetings in the introductory meeting or at any time thereafter. However, the consultant can also raise the subject after enough observation to understand the potential client meeting framework and dynamics.
3. Qualifications. The client and consultant should discuss ways that each can enhance the quality of the interactions. The consultant may wish to have an outside person brought in to assist in upgrading meetings (more is said on this later).
4. Contractual arrangements. Improving the quality of meetings may not be an explicit part of a consultant's contracted duties. However, the time and effort spent in this auxiliary activity could well increase the performance of those tasks specified in the contract.
5. Tactics. The level of involvement in assessing the results of meetings must be worked out. Client and consultant should discuss what procedures will be used for assessing meetings, the projected consequences of the assessment, and the amount of outside involvement that may be needed.

At client meetings the consultant can either present results, demonstrate techniques, or diagnose the meeting dynamics. For this third task, the consultant can quickly understand the interaction among participants and focus on any shortcomings by observing a meeting or two. The consultant can direct his observation by creating a chart like that in table 7.3, in which he lists the responsibilities of each "actor" in the meeting for the relevant meeting steps. At a subsequent meeting, the consultant observes any difficulties or obstacles encountered by those attempting to fulfill these responsibilities. These difficulties are noted on an array similar to that of table 7.3. By comparing these two arrays, the consultant can suggest ways to conduct meetings proficiently by pointing out obstacles and suggesting ways to overcome them. Box 7.1 is an example of such a suggestion sheet.

Table 7.3. Diagnostic Sheet for Meetings

Meeting Step	Leader	Participant	Arranger	Neutral Enhancer
Perceiving the need				
Decision				
Selection of attendees				
Setting of agenda				
Preparation				
The meeting				
Debriefing				

Note: Fill in the open spaces with the appropriate duties and/or problems.

Besides the consultant, another person could be asked to objectively observe the meeting and to give feedback about its design, dynamics, and results. This outsider is usually involved in one or two meetings on an informal and voluntary basis. This person could be a colleague of the consultant, an associate of the leader from another department, or an acquaintance or friend of any person involved in the meeting who has some familiarity with how meetings are run. This person could also assist the attendees in reaching consensus on the items of the agenda.

Before deciding whether to use someone with skills in running a meeting, the client and consultant should (together) answer the following questions:

- How many meetings are held each week?
- How many meetings are regularly scheduled?
- What is the average length of a meeting?
- Is the attendance usually the same at each scheduled meeting?
- Have there been communication problems, or difficulties with the agenda, follow-up, or interpersonal relations?
- Do these problems follow some pattern? What is it?
- Have meetings become progressively less effective? Why?

If the answers to the last three questions are yes, then considering a professional meeting facilitator has some distinct merit. Such a person is trained in the psychology and management of meetings and conferences. This person can help

- Free the meeting leader to participate more,
- Increase performance of the decision maker(s),

- Shorten meeting time and increase the number of tasks accomplished,
- Build trust and motivation among participants, and
- Expedite the resolution of the issue.

Hiring a facilitator is usually inexpensive in comparison with the cost of a consulting contract, and can result in long-term benefits beyond the immediate impact on the meetings being facilitated. However, if intervention is to be successful, there are concerns that must be addressed *before* a facilitator is brought on board. Difficulties in finding a suitable facilitator, in overcoming the resistance of the group to the person or idea, and in entering into a viable working agreement could all threaten the successful use of a facilitator.

A meeting is one of the major "proving grounds" of the consulting process. It is where the consultant obtains approval to perform the subtasks necessary to move the process from one stage to the next. Therefore, improving the quality of meetings allows the consulting process to move along faster and more smoothly (This 1979). The communications process during a meeting is one area in which improvement is often needed. Since communication succeeds only when what is said is heard, all parties at a meeting must be actively and fully participating for effective communication to occur.

How can each participant expand his ability to relate to others during a meeting situation? Use of the following proven techniques will help:

- Listen to what another person says rather than plan what you are going to say.
- Verify that what you have heard is what another person said before moving on to what you want to say.
- Seek acknowledgment directly when not sure that your concerns and feelings have been heard.
- Avoid secrets. Take the risk of putting on the table what you are really thinking and feeling, rather than trying to make people figure it out. Ask that others do the same.
- Use "I" statements rather than "You" statements. Stating something by taking responsibility for it allows others to deal directly with you. For example, instead of saying, "You're wrong," say, "I don't feel the same way." Instead of "You are not listening," say, "I feel that you don't hear me."

A straightforward approach, using the above techniques, engenders a sense of trust among the participants—trust that their own honest reactions

Box 7.1. Ways to Alleviate Problems/Enhance Duties of Meetings

I. Perceiving the Need
- Have core group assigned to determine when meetings are required and for what reasons.
- Be sure that the leader and core group are clear about the focus of a meeting.

II. Decision
- Decision to hold a meeting is made by both core group and leader, rather than the leader alone.
- Modifications to meeting structure and interaction are made by group consensus.

III. Selection of Attendees
- Base selection on short rationale about each person chosen.
- Consider any outside influences.

IV. Setting the Agenda
- Understand reasons for items selected and their priority.
- Set time limits for items, discussion, and additional matters.

V. Preparation
- Match setting to type of meeting.
- Provide audiovisual aids and all necessary background or supplementary materials.
- Provide coffee, ashtrays, and appropriate amenities to foster a relaxed but purposeful environment.

VI. The Meeting
- Elicit expectations of attendees and match to agenda items.
- Group handles concerns of prior meetings first, plus any immediate problems such as late start, stragglers, or crowded conditions, so that everyone's attention can then be focused only on the immediate concerns of the meeting.

VII. Debriefing
- Are all those wanting to give feedback asked to do so?
- What will be done with the comments received?

will be heard, and trust in the directness of others. The positive results of an open interaction are to create an environment in which it is possible for people to exchange ideas and feelings, and to allow personal differences to contribute to, rather than detract from, a successful interaction. In the long run, it is the development of this kind of working relationship that leads to more productive and satisfying work (Singsen 1980).

REVIEW

At this juncture, the consultant has achieved client consensus on the issue and has defined and verified the issue's causes (using the techniques of this chapter). The consultant and consultant group now examine the issue further. If any additional information is required, it is obtained using one or more of the data-gathering techniques (detailed in the previous chapter). The consultant often takes a "breather" between the last client meeting and the examination process. A few days' hiatus results in a fresh perspective that can shorten the resolution time and improve the quality of the results. After this respite, any additional data is incorporated and the consultant reviews his knowledge of similar issues. This knowledge comes from a wide range of activities—previous consulting engagements, professional literature, insights from colleagues, and other life experiences that are brought to bear on the issue. The last category, other life experiences, adds spice to the resolution process, since often an analogy from the kitchen, ballpark, or other unlikely source will serve to clarify the issue and ground it in the reality of common human experience.

SEARCH FOR RESOLUTION PATHWAYS

I. Uncover Several Viable Alternatives

Any of these viable alternatives could resolve the issue. Box 7.2 shows the brainstorm method of arriving at the alternatives to be considered. The method is a direct extension of the procedure for defining the issue (discussed in the skills section of chapter 6). The consultant is trying to accomplish three connected tasks at this point:

1. To generate a wide range of possible alternatives from the issue definition information
2. To include any alternatives the client or consultant has heretofore discussed or tried
3. To create and execute a decision framework for narrowing and choosing among the alternatives

The first task has been amply demonstrated by the issue definition example of chapter 6. A sample issue with some feasible alternatives is found in box 7.3.

II. Choose from the Viable Alternatives

Given the stated alternatives of box 7.3, how can the client choose among them?

Box 7.2. Finding Alternatives to Resolve the Issue

1. Repeat the issue definition and include causes to the issue.
2. Brainstorm various alternatives.
3. Has the client considered alternatives? If so, what are they?
4. Has the consultant considered alternatives? If so, what are they?
5. Deduce a set of feasible alternatives.
6. What are the key variables describing each alternative?
7. What kind of a decision framework is to be developed for the client?

Again, there are three tasks to be performed:

1. Extract the variables common to all of the alternatives
2. Obtain data for each variable that relates to each alternative
3. Formulate an array of variables versus alternatives to examine the relative impacts of each alternative

Table 7.4 shows how each alternative is made up of distinct variables. Each variable has an activity range associated with it. The boundaries encompass the limits of all the alternatives. For instance, to upgrade the information-handling capabilities of airline reservation offices, the client management needs results in a year or less. Of the alternatives generated in box 7.3, the fastest modifications are hypothesized to take three months. So, the range for this variable, *time frame*, is three months to a year (as shown in table 7.4). Another variable to be considered is the pres-

Box 7.3. Possible Alternatives to an Issue

Sample issue: Decrease in the quality of information transfer among airline reservation offices

Causes:
Large increase in demand for reservation services
Old telephone equipment
New airline routes and cities served
Antiquated reservation procedures

Alternatives:
A.1: Overhaul of existing telecommunications equipment
A.2: Overhaul of existing equipment plus reservation procedures
A.3: New telecommunications equipment
A.4: New telecommunications equipment plus new reservation procedures
A.5: Make no changes other than those consistent with status quo

Table 7.4. Key Variables of the Alternatives (Applied to Sample Issue in Box 7.3)

Organization	Labor	Time Frame	Price
Modify (unit, system) Produce new (unit, system)	External (1–5 people) Internal (10–15 people)	(3–12 months)	($400–$1,000/month)

Resources	Constraints	Resistances	
Available (scarce–plentiful)	Legal (none) Regulatory (0–2)	Management (some–many) Labor (few–some)	

ence of any *institutional constraints.* These are laws, rules and procedures, or regulations which may inhibit any suggested modification to the reservation system. As presented in table 7.4, there are no legal barriers to operating reservation systems, but there may well be some federal and state regulations that must be complied with when instituting certain changes.

Once the variables and their ranges have been ascertained, then the consultant seeks data supporting the variables in terms of each alternative. (The data-gathering techniques of chapter 6 are appropriate here.) With this data, an array can be constructed showing the actual variable information for the alternatives under consideration. This is illustrated in table 7.5. For example, to overhaul the *existing* reservations equipment and implement *new* reservations procedures (alternative A.2) would require six months' time and 11 people (4 outside, 7 inside), at a cost of $3,600. The people and maintenance materials needed to complete the job are readily available. If this alternative is chosen, the new procedure will be piloted and vetted in federal and state arenas, which means that new staff will have to be hired for a short time. Neither management nor labor views the hiring of temporary personnel favorably.

III. Apply a Decision Procedure

Given the alternative/variable array of table 7.5, the next step is to apply a decision procedure to choose alternatives that have the most acceptable trade-offs. "Trade-off" is the key word here: the consultant is trying to find alternatives that will work with the least amount of drawbacks, since none of the possibilities is likely to be ideal in every respect.

The decision procedure consists of both quantitative and qualitative judgments. The quantitative aspect ranks the alternatives. There are many ways to do a rank ordering, but one of the more common is an additive utility approach (Combs 1969).

First, a two-dimensional array is created, listing across the page the variables associated with each alternative, and listing down the page each alternative (as in table 7.5). Another array is then designed like the first. Based on the client's opinion of the variable's importance, a subjective weight (number) is placed above each variable. The weight has a range of values, in this case, from 1 to 10. These weights (w') are determined independent of any alternative. In the cells of the array, the client also weighs the importance of each variable to the particular alternative. These weights (v) have a range, also from 1 to 10 in the sample issue (although the range need not be the same as the w). The weights are shown generically in table 7.6 and as an example in table 7.7.

Next, a composite score for each alternative is formed from the weighting numbers. To do this, each alternative weight, v, is multiplied by each

Table 7.5. Assembling the Alternatives to Resolving Sample Issue

Alternatives	Time Frame	Internal Labor	External	Price	Resources	Constraints	Management Resistances	Labor Resistances
A.1	3 months	2 people	2 people	$400/mo	Easily available	None	Many	Few
A.2	6 months	7 people	4 people	$600/mo	Easily available	1	Many	Some
A.3	7 months	5 people	3 people	$800/mo	Mostly available	1	Many	Some
A.4	11 months	14 people	5 people	$1,000/mo	Mostly available	2	Some	Some
A.5	indefinite	0 people	1 person	$100/mo	—	None	Many	Few

Table 7.6. Weights Used in Assessing Resolution Alternatives

	w_1	w_2	w_3	w_4	w_5	w_6	w_7	w_8
Alternatives	Time Frame	Internal Labor	External Labor	Price	Resources	Constraints	Management Resistance	Labor Resistance
A.1[b]	v_{11}	v_{12}	v_{13}	v_{14}	v_{15}	v_{16}	v_{17}	v_{18}
A.2[c]	v_{21}	v_{22}	v_{23}	v_{24}	v_{25}	v_{26}	v_{27}	v_{28}
A.3	v_{31}	v_{32}	v_{33}	v_{34}	v_{35}	v_{36}	v_{37}	v_{38}
A.4	v_{41}	v_{42}	v_{43}	v_{44}	v_{45}	v_{46}	v_{47}	v_{48}
A.5	v_{51}	v_{52}	v_{53}	v_{54}	v_{55}	v_{56}	v_{57}	v_{58}

Variable Weights[a]

[a] w_1 to w_8 have a value from 1 to 10, independent of the alternatives.
[b] v_{11} to v_{18} have a value from 1 to 10 based on alternative 1.
[c] v_{21} to v_{28} have a value from 1 to 10 based on alternative 2, and so forth.

Table 7.7.   **Weights Used to Assess Resolution Alternatives in Sample Issue**

				Variable Weights			
7	4	5	5	3	2	8	4
Time Frame	Internal Labor	External Labor	Price	Resources	Constraints	Management Resistances	Labor Resistances
Alternatives							
A.1	8	6	7	7	7	9	3	7
A.2	7	7	7	7	7	7	5	5
A.3	7	7	7	7	5	7	3	5
A.4	5	3	5	6	5	5	7	3
A.5	0	0	3	10	0	9	3	7

variable weight, w, then added together. A generic representation and example are shown in table 7.8. The composite scores are then ranked from highest to lowest. The alternative corresponding to the highest value is then chosen. From table 7.9 this would be alternative A.2: to "overhaul existing equipment and add new reservation procedures."

This decision procedure has some shortcomings. First, it requires that subjective and qualitative judgments be assigned a single numerical value, which could be misleading.

There is certain tediousness in demarcating between the numbers seven and eight, between one variable and another, and sometimes between alternatives. Also, a variable weight could have a different emphasis than an alternative weight. In table 7.7, the variable "management resistances" has a high value relative to the other variables. Yet the alternative weights under this variable are greater with less management resistances.

Another possible problem with this procedure is that with a large number of alternatives, it could become unwieldy. One way to deal with this problem is to form and weight smaller, similar subgroups of alternatives within a complex issue. Then, the choices from all the subgroups would be ordered.

Although there are several variations to the additive utility approach, the shortcomings discussed above apply to other methods as well. Therefore, this procedure alone is not sufficiently reliable to provide enough information upon which to base an informed decision. It is unrealistic to assume that a client decision is founded solely on objective factors—there are other elements that enter into the decision process that are not so easily quantifiable, although no less important (Rowe 1974). The personal predilections and priorities of the people involved must be taken into account, and this requires "judgment calls" on the part of the consultant to evaluate their relative importance. Table 7.10 explores some of these qualitative factors and their likely impact on each of the alternatives in our example. Adding these "soft" factors into the decision process could uncover additional alternatives, which can either be weighted and evaluated using the additive utility approach, or discarded as being less than practical solutions.

IV. Present the Decision Procedures to the Client

The procedures derived in part III are next presented to the client and client group. The consultant explains the decision framework and suggests that time be taken by the client to ponder the alternatives, using the decision chart outlined in table 7.11. After enough time has passed for feedback and contemplation within the client group, the consultant returns for another meeting in which the desired alternative(s) are chosen.

Table 7.8. Composite Scores for Each Alternative

Alternative	Generic Score	Sample Issue Score	Composite Score
A.1	$(w_1 \times v_{11} + w_2 \times v_{12} + w_3 \times v_{13} + w_4 \times v_{14} + w_5 \times v_{15} + w_6 \times v_{16} + w_7 \times v_{17} + w_8 \times w_{18})$	$(7 \times 8 + 4 \times 6 + 5 \times 7 + 5 \times 7 + 3 \times 7 + 2 \times 9 + 8 \times 3 + 4 \times 7)$	241
A.2	$(w_1 \times v_{21} + w_2 \times v_{22} + w_3 \times v_{23} + w_4 \times v_{24} + w_5 \times v_{25} + w_6 \times v_{26} + w_7 \times v_{27} + w_8 \times v_{28})$	$(7 \times 7 + 4 \times 7 + 5 \times 7 + 5 \times 7 + 3 \times 7 + 2 \times 7 + 8 \times 5 + 4 \times 5)$	242
A.3	$(w_1 \times v_{31} + w_2 \times v_{32} + \ldots + w_8 \times v_{38})$	$(7 \times 7 + 4 \times 7 + \ldots + 4 \times 5)$	220
A.4	$(w_1 \times v_{41} + w_2 \times v_{42} + \ldots + w_8 \times v_{48})$	$(7 \times 5 + 4 \times 3 + \ldots + 4 \times 3)$	195
A.5	$(w_5 \times v_{51} + w_5 \times v_{52} + \ldots + w_8 \times v_{58})$	$(7 \times 0 + 4 \times 0 + \ldots + 4 \times 7)$	135

Table 7.9.   Decision Action on Alternatives Assessment Procedure

Alternative	Composite Score	Rank Order	Selection
A.1	241	2	
A.2	242	1	*
A.3	220	3	
A.4	195	4	
A.5	135	5	

*As a result of the above summary, A.2 is the alternative selected.

After selecting a resolution pathway, the consultant asks for the go-ahead to formulate an implementation plan for the chosen alternative(s). At the meeting, he presents for discussion a plan to put the alternatives into action. During this meeting, the consultant should also discuss the scope of the assignment with the client. Agreement needs to be reached on the nature of the specific tasks to be performed by the consultant, and a procedure discussed for handling tasks outside of the scope of the agreement. Otherwise, the resolution of the issue can be delayed, if, for example, a client repeatedly requests services that are outside the implementation boundaries of the assignment. If the scope of the assignment is defined beforehand, the consultant can simply let the client know when a request is not part of the assignment and suggest that it be dealt with after the main tasks are completed (Levesque 1973).

SPECIAL TOPIC: ISSUE RESOLUTIONS

The issue-resolution process is not always an objective and methodical one. Digressions from a straightforward approach are a natural part of the problem-solving process: indeed, as was pointed out earlier, often the insights that come from seemingly unrelated activities will help to solve a particularly difficult problem. Yet, some nontraditional ways of gaining insight into the client issue are often considered taboo in a business context. Some assumptions which could hinder rather than help resolve the issue include the following:

- Issue resolution is serious business and humor is out of place.
- Fantasy and reflection are a waste of time and energy.
- Reason, logic, and practicality are good; feeling, intuitive judgment, and theory are bad.
- Distractions should be avoided.
- Criticism should be given sparingly or not at all.
- Any issue can be resolved by the scientific method and lots of money (Adams 1976).

Table 7.10. Qualitative Aspects of Resolution Alternatives of Sample Issue

Aspect	Definition	Impacts on Alternatives				
		A.1	A.2	A.3	A.4	A.5
Advantages	Qualities that client would appreciate	Uniform procedures applied Cost effective Minimal changes in current procedures	Increased reservation volume More productive reservation personnel Changes standardized	Increased reservation efficiency Potential expanded for further sales growth Increased level of service	Increased reservation effectiveness Potential expanded for further sales Increased quality of service	No change to system Inexpensive
Disadvantages	Constraints that client could face	May not allow for new information flow May not correct employee difficulties Equipment may not be in new cities served	May not increase reservation capacity Difficulties with new ways applied to old equipment May not be cost effective	Potential conflict between new equipment and old procedures Require careful selection of equipment May not be cost effective	Matching of new equipment with new procedures Require careful selection of equipment May not be cost effective	Service quality declines Equipment maintenance cost rises Potential loss in sales

Attribute	Description					
Divisibility	Degree to which alternative can be tried on limited basis first	high	high	moderate	moderate	low
Reversibility	Degree to which status quo can be returned to if alternative not used	high	moderate	moderate	moderate	high
Risk	Previous application(s) alternative	many	some	some	few	many
Compatibility	How well alternatives fit organizational goals and client values.	poor	excellent	good	good	poor
Communicability	Relative ease of understanding and using alternative. Also, relative ease In developing an implementation plan	high	high	moderate	moderate	low

Table 7.11. Decision Chart for Resolution Alternatives

Part One—Summary

Potential Alternatives	Quantitative Score	Qualitative Score	Comments
1.	1.	1.	1.
2.	2.	2.	2.
3.	3.	3.	3.

Part Two—Choice

Potential Alternatives	Reasons for Acceptance	Reasons for Rejection	Disposition
1.	1.	1.	1.
2.	2.	2.	2.
3.	3.	3.	3.

By freeing himself from preconceived notions of what the issue resolution process *should* be, the consultant cultivates an environment that is conducive to the creative use of all his faculties to resolve the issue.

Case Example 7.1. Resolution Pathways via Behavioral Management

BCE is a small electronics manufacturing company located in a rural area of the Midwest. There has been an increasing rate of employee turnover during the last five years, to the point where half the company's workforce is being replaced every two years. Ted Clark, the vice president for administration, became aware of the problem two years ago, but, in his words, "was not able to move on it." However, recent loss in productivity and sales renewed his concern, as he suspected the decline was connected to the employee exit rate. Realizing that the corporate group was still unconcerned about the turnover rate, Clark knew he needed assistance from outside the company. He called the regional American Society for Training and Development Chapter and was given the name of a human resource development specialist in employee turnover. As he dialed the number of Jim Siegel, the specialist, Clark reassured himself that he was embarking on a correct though probably unpopular course of action.

Siegel and he met the following week at a restaurant near the firm. Clark quickly but cogently briefed Siegel on the turnover situation. Siegel remarked that it was not an uncommon problem and proposed an approach to the issue. First, Siegel recommended three articles for Clark to read on current management approaches to the turnover problem.

Next, he suggested another meeting between himself and Clark to discuss these articles in the context of the present situation. Subsequent to this meeting, a plan of action would be drawn up.

Two weeks passed. BCE lost and gained three more employees. At their next meeting, Ted Clark and Jim Siegel decided that the first step was to determine the causes for the turnover, and then find ways to stop it or slow it down. A questionnaire was distributed to employees and former employees (of two years or less) who could be located. They were asked to assess their reasons and motivations for staying with or leaving the company. The respondents were also asked to suggest ways to create a more work-conducive environment.

Most people that were contacted completed the questionnaire. The answers were tabulated and ordered by frequency of response. A summary sheet was produced by Siegel and given to Clark. It showed the employees' perceptions of the major causes of employee turnover, and the changes that would have to be made to keep them working for BCE. The vice president discussed these findings with Jim Siegel, including the likely impact on the company if they executed any of the proposed changes. From the discussion and summary sheet, Siegel prepared a decision package outlining all the options and their ramifications. Ted Clark then chose the resolution pathways to be followed.

Siegel's method has reaped results. Employee turnover has dropped to a small percentage of the total workforce. Also, recently an agreement was completed that gave labor a much larger share of responsibility in the management and day-to-day operations of the firm.

REVIEW AND EXTENSION

This chapter has been concerned with decision making in the consulting context. The purpose of the consulting effort at this stage is to define

---

Box 7.4. Search for and Discovery of Resolution Pathways

Defining the Issue
- Obtain information and insights about client issue
- Organize information in way(s) amenable to finding causes of client issue.

Generating Alternatives
- Generate alternatives using issue definition technique
- Identify variables common to every alternative
- Construct chart showing variable data for every alternative

Evaluating Alternatives
- Construct quantitative decision procedure
- Apply procedure to evaluate alternatives
- Rank-order analyzed alternatives

Choosing the Best Alternative
- Design qualitative list of factors
- Apply list to rank-ordered alternatives
- Choose desired alternatives

for the client a small number of feasible options to resolve the issue at hand. Methods for uncovering the fullest range of alternatives were explored, and they are summarized in box 7.4. Standards that reflect the client's priorities are established as criteria for choosing among these alternatives. The catalyst to this process is feedback—the constant give-and-take that keeps the assignment moving toward a resolution that is satisfactory to all.

Once an alternative is chosen as the best possible course of action in a given set of circumstances, the next step is to consider all the ways in which the proposed changes will affect every facet of that organization. This phase requires time and effort—time for reflection on all the possible ramifications of the proposed changes and effort to overcome the resistance that is an inevitable concomitant of change. This is the topic of the next chapter: learning to make the decision your own and to cope with it.

Chapter 8

Implementing the Chosen Pathway

OVERVIEW

The previous seven chapters have described a process of preparation for change. The struggle to gain a picture of the issue and to design a resolution pathway is subservient to the main thrust of the consulting engagement: realizing the needed changes. This requires that the changes be carried out and accepted as an intrinsic part of the organization's functions. This chapter and the next one cover the ramifications of change for the organization, the client-consultant relationship, and future consulting engagements.

The focus of this chapter is on the design and preliminary execution of the implementation plan. The elements of the implementation plan are discussed, and the presentation of the plan to the client is described. The early steps of the actual implementation are covered and likely obstacles are examined. A skills section is included to illuminate the two major barriers to implementation: resistance to change and lack of conflict resolution.

Change describes a state of flux, a lack of absolutes. Change is as much about loss as it is about gain: it requires a release of rigid expectations, self-limiting boundaries, and self-doubts.

By accepting the fact that we do not have all the answers, we are free to seek them out with the capabilities that we do have. Relinquishing the security of the familiar way will give us the confidence that growth (personal and organizational) occurs through change.

These assumptions need not be explicitly stated as part of a consulting contract. But, by recognizing them at the start of the engagement, they will evolve to the full point of readiness by the implementation stage.

Even if they are not perceived until the implementation stage, they can still help create an organizational climate that is amenable to change.

SKILLS SECTION

I. Resistance to Change

Change is defined either as a modification of the status quo or as the substitution of one thing for another. *Resistance* is defined (in this context) as behavior which serves to oppose.

Therefore, *resistance to change* is any conduct (primarily by the client) which seeks to maintain the status quo in the face of pressure by the consultant to alter it (Zaltman 1977).

In an organization, resistance to change can come from many sources. Some of the origins and reasons for resistance to change are listed below:

- Lack of involvement in the change process
- Threat to one's position posed by the change
- Conformity to group norms, rituals, or taboos
- Rejection by outsiders
- Fear of making a mistake
- Fear of loss of prestige
- Inability to tolerate ambiguity
- Ineffective rewards/incentives for all those affected
- Lack of resources and techniques to handle change (Walsh 1973; Adams 1976; Merry 1977; G. Lippett 1978)

What initial problems create resistance to change? The origin of the resistance may vary, but the result is usually the same. Some difficulties which are likely to lead to a later resistance to change follow:

1. Latent or initial ill feelings. Hostility toward the consultant may surface when the client does not want to make any changes or to use the consultant's services in the first place. It may also emerge if the client is not given a choice about which consultant to employ, or if he dislikes the chosen consultant. These sentiments can remain beneath the surface until changes are implemented, at which time they are likely to harden into resistance. The initial feelings can then become self-fulfilling prophecies as the consulting process proceeds.

2. Emerging dislike or disdain. Although the client may have positive feelings at first for the consultant, the consultant's actions can germinate and sustain negative feeling which may not surface until the implementation stage has begun.

3. Single incident. The client's acceptance of the consultant may be high until a specific incident changes the client's impression. The incident can be subtle or overt, can come from one-on-one interaction or group interaction, or can be related to the results of the consultant's efforts rather than to the personal interchange between the two.

4. Outside influence. Without the consultant's knowledge, the client has discussed the engagement with someone in his organization or elsewhere. After the discussion, the impression the client has of the consultant or his work is less than favorable.

5. Infighting. The client and client group are at odds over the scope and magnitude of change. This friction can create hostility toward the consultant and block any change actions.

See table 8.1 for pairings of the sources of resistance with their likely results in the consulting process.

There is no single correct strategy to overcome resistance to change, nor are there standard times or stages in the consulting process where resistance can be predicted. But it is most likely to become a stumbling block once the changes actually begin and the client is confronted with the reality of a shifting status quo.

The consultant deals with resistance to change in the context of a specific situation. Therefore, he must

1. Acknowledge the resistance. Most resistance to change is directed to the change agent—the consultant. If the client does not openly discuss his reservations with the consultant, the consultant must clearly communicate his intention to address the resistance as a discrete and separate element.

2. Find assumptions about resistance. Instead of fighting it, the consultant should begin with the assumption that some resistance is beneficial to inducing change. It is not always desirable to try to "head it off at the pass"; indeed, often the consultant should not intervene until a full airing of the client resistance is possible (if the client has not already taken care of it). In the meantime, the consultant tries not to antagonize the client about such resistance, so that it can be effectively dealt with in an environment of mutual cooperation.

3. Use strategies. The consultant takes note of instances when client resistance surfaces, the form it takes, and the changes it undergoes as the consulting process progresses. He can then choose the best strategy for dealing with it (from those developed in chapter 5) in order to set a tone that permits an open discussion of the reasons for the resistance.

Table 8.1. Elements of Resistance to Change

	Manifestation in Consulting Process				
Source	Latent or Initial Ill Feelings	Emerging Dislike	Single Incident	Outside Influence	Infighting
Lack of involvement with change		1			2
Threat to position, power, or authority	1				2
Conformity to group norms or rituals	1	2			
Rejection of outsider		1	2		
Fear of making a mistake	1				2
Inability to tolerate ambiguity		2	1		
Ineffective incentives		1	2		
Lack of preparation					2
Lack of resources				1	2

Key: 1 = primary occurrence; 2 = secondary occurrence

The consultant uses these tactics to find the resistance and to understand how the client is handling it. He can then use one or more strategies to air and overcome it. Attempts to resolve the resistance may take several consultant-client encounters or the use of multiple strategies in a single confrontation. It may never be fully resolved to everyone's satisfaction.

Each situation is different and requires a tailored approach. Thus, flexibility and openness to the circumstances of the client are necessary to effectively overcome client resistance.

Case Example 8.1. Resistance on the Firing Line

Situation: Simon Brunel has been called in by Rebecca Pasler to untangle some problems she has encountered in managing the personnel department of a department store chain. "It appears," she said, "that the difficulties are steadily mounting and I need a shovel before I'm buried. You're it."

History: Brunel did some checking into the firm's operations. He found that there had been five directors of personnel in five years, but that the company continues to expand even as its personnel policies falter. Pasler has used four outside consultants in the last six months. Brunel surmises that there may be two issues here—the personnel director and the personnel function.

Current Involvement: At his next meeting with Pasler, Brunel was greeted with "Oh, I see you've already taken the situation in hand, and without my permission, right?" Brunel responded by saying that they agreed he would gather background information on the issue. "Yes, but background information doesn't mean snooping around. OK?" Brunel nodded. After further dialogue, Pasler decided that Brunel should assess the effectiveness of the personnel department in relation to the rest of the company. Next, he should make some recommendations for viable, short-term improvements within the personnel department.

Brunel soon presented his findings to her along with a plan of action to improve the functioning of the personnel department. She agreed to all of his recommendations. After three weeks, Brunel met with her to assess his change efforts. "How's it been going, Mr. Brunel?" she asked. Brunel proceeded to detail the changes in procedures he was implementing, the feedback from the department personnel and from the whole company, and what he saw as the most likely next steps. "Well, yes, it certainly appears you have everything well under control," she said. "Please proceed, Mr. Brunel."

Two weeks later, Brunel received a call at the end of a busy day. "Brunel—this is Ms. Pasler. Can you get over here right away?"

"What's the matter?" Brunel inquired.

"Look, I have no time to talk with you on the phone. Come to my office."

"I'll be over shortly," he agreed. Upon entering Pasler's office, Brunel saw her writing furiously at a messy desk. "What seems to be wrong?" Brunel asked quietly.

"Wrong? Wrong, oh, nothing is wrong except the personnel department is coming down around me, thanks to you. You asked one of my assistants to devise a new employee data sheet. What the hell is 'data'?"

"Your employee, Ms. Prichett, and I calmly discussed what should be contained in the form. The last time I checked, she seemed to have it developed and in use."

"Well look, Brunel, I'm sick and tired of other people telling my people how to do things, not involving me, and even trying to take over. I won't have it."

Brunel was tempted to say to her, "You can have it, all right!" Instead, he confronted her with the history of the department, her use of consultants, and the fact that the company has made money not because of, but in spite of this department. Brunel pointed out that she is resistant to the changes she initially agrees to, sees outsiders as a threat to her authority, and uses a standoffish, hypercritical attitude to drive away anyone who tries to resolve the personnel problem. "Change is not easy. But it can be done. It can be successful. And, it can be liked. The decision is yours, Ms. Pasler."

Results: Within two weeks the first departmental meeting since Pasler became director took place. Brunel helped Pasler prepare for the meeting, concentrating on improving her ability to stimulate and receive feedback from those in attendance. "Wanting to learn how to communicate better is the key to your success," Brunel told her.

The events sketched in this example show that client resistance rarely takes one form and usually requires some kind of confrontational stance by the consultant to break down the barriers to change. Subsequent interaction between client and consultant reinforces the joint commitment to change, in word and in deed.

II. Conflict Resolution

When people disagree and are struggling with that disagreement, they are said to be in conflict. Disagreements can arise from many sources. They can be directly related to the object of the disagreement or they can be a transference from some other unresolved incident. They can affect a single individual or an entire organization. Conflicts can be resolved in ways ranging from informal consensus to formal, adjudicated proceedings. In the consulting context, client conflicts generally arise between client and client group, client and consultant, or client and consultant groups.

There are two types of factors that cause conflict: *interpersonal* and *process*. Interpersonal factors that could cause a clash include values, rituals, varying opinions of how to proceed, residue from prior encounters, attitudes about each other, personal benefit to be gained, and so forth. Conflict arising from the process factor stems from differing points of view on the handling of any stage in the consulting assignment, from issue definition to resolution and implementation. For either interpersonal or process factors, there is a certain, generic evolution to a conflict. The evolution is as follows:

1. Preconceived notions, which are stated or unstated assumptions on the part of the client. They are primarily expectations of how others should behave and reflect personal values and intuitions about likely behavior of others in a given situation.
2. Past experience. The preconceived notions are reinforced through everyday job experiences. These notions thus create client expectations of how others should behave.
3. Thwarted ability. Client abilities are not commensurate with the demands of the situation. The client's unrealistic expectations for himself and the consultant result in a poorly handled situation.
4. Conflict inducement. The client's insecurity shows and he attempts to thwart the consultant's actions.
5. Conflict mushroom. The tension and anxiety quickly become the focus of the interaction. Both parties argue and possibly break off communication.
6. Standoff. Both parties to the conflict are in a state of hostility toward each other. Yet, both are on the brink of inducing organizational change.

This scenario will vary with the situation—for instance, the dynamics in a group situation may differ. Also, full-scale conflict can often be avoided by the effective use of feedback to release tension and insecurities. Timing and empathy are the key factors to using feedback successfully, so that hostility need never threaten the client-consultant relationship. Nevertheless, this anatomy of a conflict presents a continuum of factors that are usually present when conflict emerges.

Some techniques to resolve client-consultant conflict are summarized in table 8.2 and are detailed below.

Mediation—This technique involves allowing a third party to act impartially with those in conflict to resolve their differences. The mediator must have the trust and support of each party and be able to get them together and listen fairly to each of them. He acts as a catalyst in settling the dispute through compromise. The mediator remains neutral throughout the

Table 8.2. Elements of Conflict Resolution

	Resolution Methods				
Cause	Mediation	Arbitration	Committee Resolution	Positive Reinforcement	Consensus
Interpersonal Factors					
Values	2			1	
Rituals	2				1
Operating philosophy	1		2		
Prior philosophy	1			2	
Encounters					
Attitude about each other	2			1	
Personal gains	2	1			
Process Factors					
Decision-making method	2	1			2
Type of consultant retained	1		1		
Issue definition given	2				2
Issue resolution given					1
Data-gathering method		1			1
Way of conducting meetings				1	
Lack of sufficient communication	2			1	2

Key: 1 = first choice of method to be used; 2 = second choice of method to be used (Note: The methods can also be used in combination).

negotiations and seeks to elucidate aspects and ideas about the conflict which neither side may have considered. The final outcome of the conflict lies with the parties in dispute, who gradually move from mutually exclusive positions to a compromise that accommodates both positions.

Arbitration—This technique is similar to mediation, with this difference: an arbitrator has the authority to decide the dispute if the parties involved cannot, and he may side with either party. The arbitrator, chosen by the parties in conflict, listens to both sides of the dispute, then attempts to make a decision that will be as fair as possible to all concerned.

Committee resolution—This technique is used primarily but not exclusively with groups. A few people are selected from the client and consultant groups, and are given the responsibility to work through the conflict. This committee collects information about the dispute; calls in outsiders for assistance, if necessary; and persuades those directly in conflict to seek compromise of their differences. An effective committee needs a clear mandate to carry out its functions and must not be covertly trying to subvert resolution. The recommendations the committee makes to the larger group should be accepted as the resolution.

Group processes—Here the client and consultant groups are in conflict. There are various group processes that could be used, one of which is *positive reinforcement*. After the conflict has been aired, an outsider is called in to work with the groups. He stimulates interaction through activities that reinforce positive feelings among group members. These activities could include ordinary conversation about things not related to the dispute, playing noncompetitive games together, role-playing to better understand each other's situation, studying together, and so forth. The objective in each case is to achieve friendly rapport within each group and between the two groups.

Consensus—This technique is used to settle intergroup conflict as well as disputes between an individual and a group. It is similar to mediation, although here it is used in a group setting. An objective observer acts to facilitate open discussion of grievances by all parties. The observer helps to air all sides of the conflict and works with the groups to formulate proposals for resolving the conflict. Discussion continues on the proposals until consensus is reached on a course of action. When objections are raised, they are fully discussed and the results of those discussions are usually incorporated into the compromise resolution.

Whoever performs the function of directing the conflict toward resolution, the uninvolved party should be responsible and able to bring about an expedient and fair settlement.

Resistance to change is primarily directed from the client to the consultant. As such, the consultant not only tries to facilitate change but also tries to work through any personal resistance. To reach mutual consent, the consultant must sustain credibility with the client on both the personal and professional levels. The previously established rapport is called upon to help find the sources of the resistance and ways of overcoming it. The use of strategies and feedback will relieve some of the tension and anxiety about the change.

The *conflict resolution* process can be used at any point in the consulting assignment. Unlike *resistance to change*, it is not only directed from the client to the consultant but can also be found between or among any of the people involved. The conflict need not grow and stew as with resistance to change, but can be directly and immediately dealt with. Working through resistance to change requires consultant feedback, client willingness, and the joint use of one or more consulting strategies. The resolution of a conflict is accomplished by the consultant choosing one or more techniques, gaining client consent, and fully implementing the technique(s).

In either case, the end of the episode results in a higher level of cooperation and trust.

DEVELOPMENT OF THE IMPLEMENTATION PLAN: PRELUDE

The consultant now reviews the client's mandate to begin developing the implementation plan. The review is begun by carefully assessing the boundaries of the plan, incorporating the consultant's own sense of the tasks to be done, and matching the tasks to the client perception of the resolved issue. One way to minimize resistance to change when presenting the plan is to first discuss low-risk tasks that have easily predictable results and broad-based support, and then move to higher-risk tasks that have less obvious results and are likely to meet with stronger resistance. By first engaging the client's interest and involvement in noncontroversial issues, a working relationship develops that has greater flexibility for accommodating change and potential disagreements without disruption. A plan will be far more likely to gain the interest and personal involvement of the client if it invites his input. Allowing enough leeway in the plan for new data, critiques and suggestions, and possibly new tasks will increase the likelihood of client acceptance (Lebell 1973).

DEVELOPMENT OF THE IMPLEMENTATION PLAN: INTERLUDE

The implementation plan essentially says what is to be done, who is to do it, how it will be accomplished, and any consequences if it is not done. It consists of the following elements:

Overview—The history of the issue is highlighted and the issue is defined. The resolution pathway is briefly described and an explanation is given for why it was chosen. The objectives of the plan are specified.

Activities—Each of the steps activating the plan is described. The types of tasks and subtasks are noted, along with their expected results.

Resource utilization—The personnel needed for each task are specified. The time frame for the implementation is given on a step-by-step basis. The needed resources are detailed, and any budgetary adjustments are requested.

Administration—The means of monitoring the overall progress of the plan is covered, along with any possible side effects or contingencies. This includes specifying the order of the implementation steps (whether concurrent, sequential, or additive), the communication links among the steps, and the handling of side issues (Kilmann 1979).

Impacts of change—All the likely ramifications of change are discussed, including the impact on the client group, the larger organization (if any), and the outside world. Ways of preparing people for change are detailed, along with a plan for dealing with resistance to change. The effects of the changes on the long-term goals of the organization, and any likely modification of these goals are hypothesized. Possible shortcomings of the plan are included (Kubr 1976; Jackson 1975).

DEVELOPMENT OF THE IMPLEMENTATION PLAN: POSTLUDE

The written plan is polished and made ready for oral presentation to the client. The presentation should have a "dry run" in the consultant's shop before its debut to the client.

When the plan is finally presented, the consultant should be open to feedback from the client and be able to address any immediate client barriers or friction that may arise. At this time, a person is designated by the client to serve as client liaison and work closely with the consultant and/or consultant group during the implementation of the plan.

IMPLEMENTATION: ACTION AND CONTROL

This step is the most dynamic and most comprehensive of any discussed thus far. It is the culmination of all the effort that has preceded it and requires most of the consulting skills discussed in earlier chapters. The agreed-upon changes must be put into effect, and they must work. As discussed earlier, the outlined changes should be made incrementally.

As one subgroup has its functions altered or as one activity is tried by the entire group, a short evaluation is done. If it is successful, then the next alteration or new activity is begun. If it is not successful, then the problems are aired and remedied before the next change is put into action.

In this step, all members of the client group are apprised of the changes *before* they begin. The objective of the consultant and client is to improve the structure of the organization and the way in which the client group relates to its functions. The milieu is one of change: the prior effort invested in keeping communication channels open now results in a mutual confidence and trust that changes will be made with competence and sensitivity.

Case Example 8.2. Conflict Out of Control

Jill Byers was having a discussion over coffee with Jack Williams, supervisor of the Dilltown Plant Office of Strength Tool and Dye Co. She had been called in as a consultant by the senior vice president of the company to survey the dye mold equipment and test for any fatigue or possible fractures, based on her expertise and reputation in this area.

"No question but that my initial inspections show hairline cracks in two molds," she said to Jack.

"Jill—is two days enough time to verify these cracks? This could be a serious matter. Why, normally the equipment needs to be watched and measured for a week before anything can be found," Jack questioned.

"That's true, Jack. Normally it does take longer, and it could indeed be serious. But these cracks were relatively accessible and easy to locate," she replied.

Jack persisted, "I don't know—it just seems so quick—are you *positive*?"

"Don't worry, Mr. Williams," she replied frostily. "I know my job and I'll do it well for you."

Over the next two weeks, Jill compiled her observations of equipment operating procedures and measurements of equipment performance characteristics by working closely with the employees on the floor of the plant. She presented her findings to Jack Williams and staff at a hastily called meeting at the beginning of her fourth week there.

"Ms. Byers, I just don't see how you're able to make these findings," Jack stated.

"They are backed up by tried and tested techniques," Jill replied.

"Yes—but if what you say is true, I'm going to lose about 100 hours of production time while the equipment is repaired or even replaced. I can't afford to do it," Jack firmly stated.

"You can't afford not to," Jill said matter-of-factly.

"Look," said Jack. "If you think you're so smart, then tell us where we're going to get the funds to do these so-called repairs. The only option you've given us is the most expensive."

"I was asked to verify whether the equipment has metallurgical problems—and that's all," Jill stated.

"You bet that's all—you can take your report and leave," Jack shouted. With that, the meeting broke up.

(At this point, Jill Byers has a decision to make. Since she is a consultant hired by the senior vice president, she could merely continue her consulting, submit a report, and then submit a payment voucher. However, the possibility of future work, the challenge to expand her consulting assistance, and her interest to learn more about this company may cause her to act otherwise.)

The following week, Jill made her final recommendations based on her studies: "In conclusion, there is only one road to take—new equipment must be purchased with all possible haste." Jack Williams sat there stunned. She would now have the gall, he thought, to suggest only the most expensive option. Jack was enraged. He called the senior vice president to explain this aggravating situation. He questioned Byers's competency to make such a sweeping decision since he felt that she apparently lacked an understanding of the consequences to Strength Tool and Dye of buying and installing new equipment. Jack ended by suggesting that her services be dispensed with "immediately."

"Jack, I know how you feel," the senior vice president replied. "Although her style may seem abrasive to you, her findings are valid. Believe me, I'm the last person to want to go along with such a large expenditure if it is not necessary. But if new equipment is needed, there's nothing to be gained by delay. Besides, we have a contract for Ms. Byers's services, and she has an excellent reputation for honesty and action."

"Well, in this case, I simply cannot agree with her action," Jack stated grimly. "It looks like this company is just not big enough for Byers and me."

This case example is typical of situations many consultants find themselves in. The path which Jill Byers chose was to recognize that the supervisor has other pressures and that his concerns for these are spilling over into his communications with her but not to get involved in trying to resolve Jack's resistance to her presence and her findings. Clear understanding of the mandate and influence which a consultant can handle is a necessary requisite to a successful consultation.

Case Example 8.3. Time to Intervene, Time to Contravene

QSD, Inc., a medium-size company with roots firmly imbedded in the southwestern community of Wells, is in need of a "face-lift." RD&C, Inc., a consulting firm of national repute, was hired to conduct a needs assessment for the firm's new direction. For years, the company manufactured digital-to-analog converters, but with declining demand, a new avenue of profit was needed.

RD&C's representative, David Prosese, was given the "green light" by QSD's board of directors to formulate a plan for entering the research and development market. David and his staff worked for three weeks and came up with an approach to changing from a production firm to a service firm providing conversion and upgrade capabilities. The written report of the plan was straightforward, interactive, and cross-referenced. Each page had a summary section at the top, and major activities broken down into key tasks in the center. The people responsible for executing the tasks were listed by title at the bottom of each page. Each activity was followed by a discussion about the impact on the existing situation, including the likely need for new staff, outside assistance, or other resources.

After all the activities were described, a separate portion of the plan was devoted to its administration, including high-level responsibilities, accountability, and quality control.

Finally, the activities were ordered chronologically and presented graphically, giving the sequence in which changes should be implemented.

David Prosese and staff came to QSD to present the plan to the board. Being a man of terse language, his explanation was over in 20 minutes. There was silence. The board members whispered to one another, and then the chairman spoke:

> I'd like to compliment you on your short, to-the-point presentation. What you gave us, we understand. However, a few comments from myself and my colleagues are in order.
>
> As a board, our main concern is effective delegation of responsibility and the results that ensue from this delegation. The tasks to be done in carrying out these responsibilities are of secondary importance. Yet your document and oral presentation reverse this priority.
>
> Second, the order of tasks leaves something to be desired. The first task listed on your view chart is to sell off the old equipment and use the capital generated as marketing funds to attract new clients. Mr. Prosese, that is fine as far as it goes, but, some of the old equipment is still usable to us during the transition phase. Further, even if we were to accrue this marketing money you speak of, who would do the marketing for us? You have shown how we'd need to hire four new people in the marketing branch, but you have not addressed the question of who would hire them and how their duties would relate to the tasks you have described. Moreover, nowhere do you mention anything about contingencies. What if we cannot find four marketing people? What if we have trouble selling the equipment? And, if this avenue for generating capital does not work, what other alternatives are open to us?

I am chairman of this board partly because of my past experience and partly because of my insight, but also of my ability to communicate. Your plan, we concur, is not well defined or properly structured and could cause much friction in its implementation. These words are said in candor and without malice. Back to the drawing board on your own time, or assume the contract is over. Which will it be, sir?

Little else needs be said about this example except that it reinforces the guidelines of the text. That is, ensure that the implementation plan is written to your audience, structured for immediate client use, and flexible enough to allow for adjustments and new inputs.

REVIEW AND EXTENSION

Until this chapter, there has been only preparation and staging for the changes about to occur. Now, change begins to move the organization. With Newtonian precision, equal and opposite forces push back on this movement in the shape of resistance to change.

Getting the client to aid rather than resist the change is the consultant's task at hand. An awareness of forces that can create and disarm conflict is a necessary tool in the consulting engagement. The exercise of careful judgment is always called for in a decision of whether or not to confront resistance or conflict head-on. Some say that under-the-surface conflict should be left alone to work out its own way. Others believe that discussions about conflicts should not be broached by the consultant for fear of losing client favor. The amount of intervention appropriate to a given situation is dependent on the consultant's experience, his ability, and the degree to which he has fostered interaction with the client. The speed at which opposing views are reconciled is indicative of the growing maturity of the client-consultant relationship, and speedy resolutions bode well for a successful completion of the engagement.

Chapter 9

Monitoring, Termination, and Evaluation

OVERVIEW

At this stage in the consulting process, the change efforts are well under way. The consultant is carrying forth the implementation scheme of the last chapter. The client is assisting the consultant's efforts by providing resources and actively participating in modifications to the organization. It is a period of intensive activity for both client and consultant. Changes are occurring within the client organization, results are beginning to emerge from these changes, and the end of the consulting assignment is in sight. The client is concerned about the outcome and hopeful for a successful one. He attempts to sustain the motivation level of the client group to make the consultant-brought changes their own.

The consultant implements the resolution plan on a step-by-step basis and, in order to ensure that the changes remain on target with the client's needs, remains open to constant discussion and frequent modification of the proposed actions. Both client and consultant must pay simultaneous attention to ironing out the details of the implementation scheme, while constructing and reinforcing the pillars of longer-term change. The balance between immediate change and long-term change is often precarious, but the mutual will to see the changes made smoothly provides the primary impetus to work out minor concerns so that they do not impede the change effort.

In this chapter the emphasis is on consultant disengagement and client-consultant closure. In the disengagement stage, the client and client group function in the changed situation without the help formerly provided by the consultant. They attempt to carry out their organizational responsibilities independent of consultant intervention. This does not mean the consultant just vanishes from the scene; rather, it means that additional consultant help on the resolved issue is kept to a minimum (Bell and Nadler 1979). This stage is also a time of evaluation of the assignment, the participants, the process, and the results.

Closure consists of two major events. One is the joint evaluation meeting where the results of each party's own evaluation are presented and discussed. The other is the consultant presentation of the final report to the client. In whatever order these occur, it is customary to end the successful consultation with some form of celebration. Thus, the objective of this stage is for consultant and client to finish the engagement and part company with the same, if not more respect than existed at the first client-consultant meeting.

SKILLS SECTION: WRITING A REPORT

This section presents techniques and underlying assumptions helpful in the reporting of the consulting engagement. First, the assumptions:

- A written report has similar elements to *any* written contact with the client. The steps detailed below are also used in abbreviated fashion when a progress report, memorandum, special position paper, or proposal is put together. However shortened, all steps need be included to produce an effective document.
- The emphasis of the report is determined by the client's attitude, understanding, and concerns at the time of composition. This cardinal principle gives primary direction to the consultant's activity.
- Different consulting engagements will have different reporting requirements. Technical assignments generally include an analysis of the issue and recommendations in written form. Behavioral assignments may have no formal written requirements, although many times the client requests a copy of the chronology and findings of the issue resolution.
- The thrust of this section is to create a written document that is clear, pertinent, and useful in the long run for reinforcing the insights learned by the client. In a sense, writing a report is a mini–consulting process in which the issue can be defined as producing a viable and timely document of the consultation. The resolution of the issue is the procedure developed below for report writing.

This section is divided into two parts: writing the report and constructing graphics.

I. Writing the Report

Much has been written and many seminars have been conducted on technical communications. The chief intent of these volumes and short courses has been to motivate the would-be communicator to write and present written information more effectively. Above all, truly effective communication is assured only if thorough feedback is an integral part of the procedure.

A *report* is a factual and sometimes interpretative presentation of information directed to a particular reader or audience to achieve a specific purpose. A report can

- Record past events,
- Convey new information,
- Analyze and structure information for decision making, and/or
- Recommend one or more courses of action.

Consulting report writing is not an inductive exercise in logic, nor is it a diary of events. Consulting writing must communicate facts of interest to the client using a dynamic and varied style. Concepts about the consulting assignment should be presented in a clear, easily understandable fashion. An effective report requires preliminary planning of the size, content, and format of the document.

How does one produce effective written communication about the consulting assignment? The pertinent steps are listed in box 9.1 and are described below:

A. Purpose Definition

Before embarking on the composition, the consultant should ask himself and, if necessary, the client, the following questions to determine if a report is justified:

- Is the report necessary? Why?
- What will the report accomplish?
- Is there a better way to accomplish the purpose?
- Is this the appropriate time for writing a report?

B. Audience Identification

Answers to the following questions will help to focus on the interest of the reader(s):

- Will the report be directed to one or many readers?
- How do the potential readers' knowledge about and involvement in the assignment vary?

Box 9.1. Major Steps to Writing a Report

A. Define the purpose of the report.
B. Identify the reader(s).
C. Structure the report.
D. Construct a detailed outline.
E. Gather and organize the data.
F. Write the first draft.
G. Edit and rewrite the draft.
H. Obtain feedback about the draft.
I. Compose the final version.
J. Print and distribute the document.

- How do the potential readers' expectations differ with respect to the results of the assignment?

Using the answers to these questions, the consultant can next determine

- The number of separate reports to be written. Should he compose a single report oriented to all intended readers or separate reports geared to each reader's viewpoint and understanding?
- The style of each report. Should the report be written in narrative, persuasive, argumentative, or chronological style?
- The kind and amount of information to include. What type of vocabulary should be used, how much background needs to be provided, and what level of detail is necessary throughout the report?

C. Report Structure

The structure of the report should reflect its contents. There are several ways to structure the material to maintain a strong focus on its purpose and audience throughout the report. Some alternatives are provided in box 9.2 (Kubr 1976). Once an appropriate structure for the report is chosen, then the general elements, or modules, in which the information is presented, are selected. The following might be included in a report:

1. *Title page.* This contains the title of this report, its authors (generally including prime and subcontractors), the client for whom the report is done, the contract number, and the date of the report.
2. *Table of contents.* This gives the outline of the report sections with respective page numbers.
3. *List of illustrations.* This provides a listing of every graphic used in the report with its corresponding page number.

Box 9.2. Alternative Structure for a Report

- *Report elements:* Description, analysis, evaluation, conclusions, recommendations
- *Subject elements (for example):* Supply, demand, production

The report could be structured in the following ways:

A. By Report Element	**B. By Subject Element**	**C. Hybrid**
Description	*Supply*	*Supply*
Supply	Description	Description
Demand	Conclusions	Conclusions
Production	Recommendations	*Demand*
Conclusions	*Demand*	Description
Supply	Description	Conclusions
Demand	Conclusions	*Production*
Production	Recommendations	Descriptions
Recommendations	*Production*	Conclusions
Supply	Description	*Recommendations*
Demand	Conclusions	Supply
Production	Recommendations	Demand
		Production

---

4. *Acknowledgments.* This is an optional page mentioning all those people directly and indirectly responsible for and contributing to the report. A graceful way of acknowledging the help of contributors while avoiding an extended listing of their names is to name only the principal contributors and mention all others in a general expression of gratitude.

5. *Abstract.* In a paragraph or two, this optional element summarizes the purpose of the report, its methodology, and results. It is geared to the client and includes the essence of any recommendations contained in the report.

6. *Executive summary.* This is probably as important as the main body of the report in terms of information value. It is also considered to be the part of the report that is most widely read by influential people. The summary encapsulates the entire report by giving brief descriptions of the main textual material. If it is a fairly short report, the executive summary could suffice as an abstract or extended abstract. It is important that the principles of clear writing articulated below be applied here.

7. *Body of the report.* See section F below.

8. *Appendices.* These sections are reserved for pertinent data, supporting documents, or explanation of principles or techniques useful

to the report, but which would disturb the flow of the report if included in its body. Such items as statistical information, related legislation, acronyms and definitions, bibliography, more in-depth analyses, supplementary graphs and charts, and so forth, are typically included here.

D. Detailed Outline

All major report sections and subsections are included in the outline. This is reviewed and discussed by the consultant team to ensure that nothing is left out of the report and that all items are in proper relation to each other. Changes may be made in this review that necessitate rewriting some sections of the report.

E. Data Acquisition and Organization

Most information about the consulting assignment is in existence at this point. All information, insights, results, and comments are arranged to fit the detailed outline. Any remaining data holes are filled as the importance of the data and time dictate.

F. Composition of First Draft

If the outline has been adequately prepared and examined, the first draft should flow easily from it. The writer of each section should address each subtopic in detail, incorporating graphics, supporting data, and insights. If more than one person is writing the report, then sections should be assigned for the first draft. If the outline has been carefully planned and executed, each person should be able to proceed with his section without concern for the way the sections will fit together. A checklist for the first draft is provided in box 9.3.

G. Report Editing

After completing a first draft, the report could be shelved for a time in order to give the writer(s) time to regain objectivity about the composition. When work is resumed, the editing of a report with many authors and an editor is usually done in two passes. The purpose of the first pass is to coordinate all of the parts into a coherent whole.

The project manager or editor takes all the written parts, graphics, and materials earmarked for appendices and connects them into a rough report. This activity entails rewriting the first and last paragraphs of each section to maintain flow and continuity. The sections are also edited for

Box 9.3. Checklist for the First Draft

1. Have all the main headings of the outline been covered?
2. Likewise, have all subheadings of the outline been covered?
3. Have relevant ideas and facts been included where needed?
4. Is there a coherent main point, subordinate point pattern?
5. Are all concepts requiring redefinition defined, and are the definitions functional?
6. Are the relationships clear, analogies appropriate, and examples helpful?
7. Are the ideas supported by substantial evidence?
8. Are there any contradictions or vague development of ideas?
9. Are there redundancies? Should they be left in for emphasis?
10. Are the conclusions cogent and supported by the report?
11. Are the recommendations concise and supported by the conclusions?
12. Is the purpose of the report well served by this exposition?
13. Is the reader of the report well served by this exposition?

consistency of tone. Finally, the report is checked for overall consistency and a logical progression of ideas.

The second pass is where the rigorous editing begins. An inductive strategy is often useful; that is, the editing process begins by looking first at words; then sentences, paragraphs, and subsections; and finally sections of the report. With each reading the report is edited to strengthen its readability by eliminating redundancies and wordiness and replacing them with succinct, clear language. Some of the steps of the inductive editing process may be incorporated into a single pass-through, as long as there is not so much attempted at a single reading that careful editing is sacrificed. The steps of the editing process are as follows:

1. *Words.* Each word is examined to determine whether it could be deleted or changed to a simpler or more precise term. Jargon and clichés are replaced by standard usage. Table 9.1 lists some unnecessarily complex or overused words and their simpler alternatives.

2. *Sentences.* A second round of editing focuses on sentences. Redundant clauses or phrases are deleted. Vague sentences are restructured to express ideas with greater clarity. Complex sentences are untangled and broken up so that one sentence expresses a single idea. Most verbs are expressed in the active voice, with an occasional switch to the passive voice for variation. Sentences can be varied through word choice, sentence structure, or length. A mixture of simple, compound, and complex sentences will contribute to a lively style and an easily understandable flow of ideas.

3. *Paragraphs.* Unity and coherence are qualities of the well-written paragraph. Unity is the development of ideas that flow from the topic

sentence of a paragraph in a sequential and consistent fashion. Connectives[1] are used to pave the way for smooth transitions from sentence to sentence and from paragraph to paragraph. Ideas expressed coherently unfold in a logical progression in short, concise sentences. Weeding out extraneous sentences is a necessary part of this stage of the editing process. Graphics or illustrations also help the reader to quickly grasp the concepts being presented, and these are checked for form, content, and their relation to the text.

4. *Subsections.* Do the paragraphs develop concepts in a sequential and explanatory manner? Are all the points to be covered in a subsection fully explained? Are there too many or too few ideas in the subsection? Changes in order, deletions, or additions of paragraphs are considered at this stage. It may be helpful to reference ideas with *blurbs* and *glosses*. A blurb is a sentence which summarizes the ideas to follow, say, in the subsection. It normally appears indented under the title of the subsection. A gloss is a clause or phrase that appears in the margin and briefly indicates what the paragraph is about (Holtz 1979). Both devices have varying success rates and depend on the length of subsection and the writer's requirement for repeating the developed ideas.

5. *Sections.* The sections of the report are reviewed for consistency with each other, for their transitions from one to another, and for additional condensation and clarification. If a section is deemed unworkable or is poorly written, another try by the writer is in order. After the new version is completed, it will be examined for fit, clarity, and conciseness.

Another aspect of the editing process is to verify that all desired ideas are in the material and are clearly and logically developed and supported. Such examination can also bring to light concepts or relationships not considered before. Their inclusion could enhance the report; however, the insights are valuable even if they are not subsequently included. Finally, it should be noted that clear, creative composition is a skill that is slowly honed by repetition of the above procedures over the course of many reports.

H. Draft Feedback

The report is circulated to the client, client group, and other interested parties. Once they review it, their comments may be shared among the group with the goal of improving its content and structure. Additional discussion could also ensue about future consulting in this issue area.

---

1. A connective is a word or words that link. Examples include "besides," that is, "in conclusion," for example, "lastly," "likewise," "therefore," "but," "on the other hand," "or," "nor," "and," and "soon."

Table 9.1.   A Guide to Simpler Usage

Instead of these words	Try these words
abortive	vain, fruitless
accommodate	fit, change, alter
acknowledge	take note of, admit
acquaint	tell
acquire	get, add, gain
adjacent	beside, next to, nearby
administer	manage, run, hand out
aggregate	total, sum, compile
alleviate	lighten, lessen, ease
along the lines of	like
ameliorate	improve, make better
appropriate	fit, proper
as a result	because, therefore
ascertain	learn, find out
as previously mentioned	as stated
assist	help
associate	link, join, unite, partner, co-worker
as soon as	when
attempt	try
at the present time	now
attitude	stand, view
cease	stop, quit
circumstance	fact, event
circumvent	baffle, foil, outwit, thwart
combine	unite, link, join
commence	begin, start
communicate	tell
component	part
conduct	do, carry out
configuration	pattern, shape
conform	agree, square, fit, tally
consequence	outcome, result
consider	study, weigh

(*continued*)

Table 9.1. (continued)

Instead of these word	Try these words
construct	build
consummate	finish, complete, perfect
contingent	accidental, likely, uncertain
correspond	agree, tally
deficient	faulty, lacking
delineate	trace, outline, picture
derive	arise, spring, stem
despite the fact that	although
determine	decide, find out
detriment	hurt, harm, loss
difficulty	trouble, hardship
disadvantage	drawback, handicap
due to the fact that	because
duplicate	copy, repeat, reproduce
dynamic	active, lively
eliminate	rule out, set aside, get rid of
enhance	increase, intensify, improve, enlarge, advance, add to, strengthen, boost, multiply
establish	found, set up
evaluate	test, appraise, rate
exceed	outdo, go beyond
facilitate	help, ease, smooth, aid, simplify, speed up
finalize	complete, finish, end
for the purpose of	to, for
function	act, work, duty, job
fundamental	basic
in accordance with	as
in a position to	can
inception	origin, root, source
increase	enlarge, grow
indicate	say, show, tell
ineffective	fruitless, vain
inefficient	wasteful
inexpensive	cheap

Table 9.1. (*continued*)

Instead of these words	Try these words
inflexible	unbending, rigid
inhibit	check, curb
initial	first, early, starting, beginning
initiate	start, begin
in order to	to
in regard to	about
institute	found, set up, start
integrate	combine
in the event that	if
introduce	insert, bring into
investigate	look into
in view of the fact that	because, since
iterate	repeat
minimize	reduce, lessen, belittle
mitigate	lighten, ease
mode	style, form
modify	change, alter
numerous	many
objective	neutral, aim, goal
obtain	get, gain, win
occur	happen
operate	act, work, run
optimum	best, most effective, realistic, practical, useful
perform	act, do, carry out
personnel	staff, workers, employees
phase	side, stage, part
position	job, place, stand
presently	now, shortly
previous to, prior to	before
proceed	come from, go on
purview	range, reach
restrain	check, curb
restrict	limit
retard	slow down, hold back

(*continued*)

Table 9.1. (*continued*)

Instead of these words	Try these words
revoke	undo, cancel
significant	meaningful, important, notable, huge, vast
simultaneous	at the same time
subject	liable, prone, person
subordinate	subject
substantial	large, real, tangible
succeed	follow, thrive, win
supplement	add to
systematic	orderly, arranged
terminate	end, finish, complete
there is the possibility that	probably, possibly
transfer	shift
transform	change
transmit	carry, send, pass along
utilize	use
validate	verify, prove
with reference to	about
with regard to	about, concerning, on

I. Composition of the Final Version

With all comments conscientiously incorporated into the text and the graphics, the report is typed and proofread for spelling, capitalization, typographical errors, organization, and content. Any final changes to the structure of the report are made, although they should be minor ones at this stage. If the consulting unit has its own format and layout, these are applied to the report. The cover is designed and the binding is selected.

J. Document Production and Distribution

The report is now reproduced, either by offset printing, photocopying, or some other printing method. If word processing software is used to prepare the report, corrections and modifications to the draft are simple and inexpensive. This, in turn, leaves funds for higher-quality reproduction. The final report is generally hand delivered and/or electronically presented to the client. Additional copies are usually made upon request.

II. Graphics and Report Enhancement

The term "graphic" refers to the representation of information or ideas by a graph or a diagram. Its function is to present specific and generally comparative information. A graphic does not communicate independently from the text. It is used to *complement* what has been written by creating visual interest and impact (Broekhuizen 1979; Weil 1978). Professional graphics are uniform in style and do *not* place too much copy on a single chart. Some commonly asked questions about the use of graphics are answered below:

A. What criteria are used to determine the need for graphics?

- The nature and purpose of the report
- The intended reader and his requirement for graphics
- The idea or data to be illustrated

B. What kinds of information should be displayed in graphic form, and how should it be presented?

A graphic serves three functions: to compare quantities, to display sequences, and to display spatial relationships. There are several ways of presenting graphics, including lists, tables, arrays, pie charts, organization charts, flowcharts, line graphs, or bar graphs. Table 9.2 shows a cross-comparison of the form and function of a graphic. As guidelines to choosing a particular graphic form, the following should be kept in mind:

- The graphic should accurately reflect the data.
- The graphic should be easily read and understood.
- The format should not distort the data.

C. How are graphics developed?

First, the report text is written. Then, the graphics are developed to supplement the text by displaying information that cannot be fully described in words. An effective graphic will

- Clarify complex ideas,
- Emphasize key points,
- Maintain continuity, and
- Be precise and succinct.

Table 9.2 Form versus Function in Graphics

Forms	Compare Quantities	Display	Show Spatial Relationships
	Functions		
List	X	X	
Table	X	X	
Array	X		X
Pie chart	X		
Organization chart	X	X	
Flowchart		X	
Line graph	X		X
Bar graph	X		X

Thus the writer and graphics designer need to consider the writer's perceptions of what graphics are desired. During this session, the following questions are reviewed:

- What are the essential concepts to be communicated?
- Which concepts can be communicated graphically?
- Which graphic form is best suited to the information?
- How much time and money are available to produce the graphics?
- How will each graphic augment the text?

D. Are the final graphics useful to the report?

The graphics are thus roughly designed and drawn. Writer and designer review the graphics in order to

- Edit the graphic so that it is uncluttered and highly legible,
- Ensure even distribution of information;
- Ensure balanced lettering;
- Check for spelling, symbol, and number accuracy; and
- Use color where it can be reproduced successfully.

The writer again notes the graphic's relation to the text and its ability to concisely add dimension to the report ideas and information.

PERFORMANCE EVALUATION

Performance evaluation requires a qualitative and quantitative assessment of how well an activity was carried out. This effort requires knowledge of the activity, an understanding of the viewpoints of those who were involved, and a sense of what could be done to make it better. While evaluation should be a part of every stage of the consulting process, it is particularly important that a full-scale performance evaluation be conducted at the end of the engagement. This should include

- The consultant's internal evaluation. As the assignment is completed, the consultant returns to his home turf and assesses the assignment with the consulting team (if any).
- The client's internal evaluation. The client assesses the consultant's abilities and activities as well as his own responses and activities in light of the new information or knowledge gained during the consulting assignment.
- Mutual dialogue on the assignment. After these two tasks are completed, client and consultant groups meet to compare notes, exchange opinions, and discuss ways to strengthen each other's position and efforts now and in the future (Shay 1974; Merry 1977).

Such a procedure could lead to future assignments for the consultant. But this remains to be seen. To find topics for examination, then, let's first discuss *errors* that consultants and clients make during the consulting assignment (these errors do not include breaches of ethics or potentially illegal actions).

Consultant errors. A sample listing of some common mistakes made by consultants is shown in box 9.4.

Client errors. Some frequent mistakes that clients make in the consulting process are shown in box 9.5.

These errors are later used by the consultant and client, respectively, as criteria for assessing the consulting assignment. The assessment is not made in a vacuum. Each party reveals its own shortcomings and focuses on how the other helped or hindered the effort. Thus, the evaluation begins.

Consultant Evaluation

The consultant, either alone or with the consulting team, assesses his performance in the engagement. The questions listed in box 9.6 are useful for this purpose. The purposes of the evaluation are to gain perspective on the assignment, to bring forth any shortcomings of the team, and to achieve consensus on how they can operate more effectively in the future. A variety of methods can be used to elicit feedback about the consultation, including role-playing, questionnaire completion followed by group discussion, or straightforward interaction. Whatever technique is used, the motivation is the same—to elicit feedback and interchange about

Box 9.4. Common Consultant Errors

- Does not include top management in changes made through the consulting process
- Tries to change more factors within the organization than can be successfully dealt with by the client and client team during the time of the consulting assignment
- Not able to discern whether the client's situation could be effectively handled by consultant's skills, orientation, and experience
- Loses objectivity and becomes more committed to the changes than to the ways in which the change sequence will occur in the organization
- Uses a marketing person to sell the client on the assignment, then has inexperienced people attempt to handle client's issue with inadequate supervision.
- Fails to develop sensitive, interactive rapport with the client
- Fails to complete the assignment within time and/or budget constraints
- Unable to make presentations which stimulate further client involvement with consultant's efforts
- Does not resolve the client's issue
- Does not fulfill the commitments made in the proposal
- Omits an evaluation of the consultation
- Conveys an "image" to the client which stifles ability to act as an agent for change (Reddin 1977; Jay 1977; Zaltman 1977)

Box 9.5. Client Errors in Consulting

- Does not attempt to define the issue or find a way to resolve it before calling in a consultant
- Unable to secure funding for a consultant
- Is not willing to be honest and direct with the consultant
- Attempts to block consultant efforts
- Gives the consultant little or no feedback
- Fails to implement consultant recommendations over the long term
- Employs the consultant to do a small, well-defined project, but then tries to informally "milk" him for help on a wide range of unrelated issues
- Does not integrate the interaction with the consultant into his management responsibilities
- Fails to make effective use of many of the techniques discussed in chapters 3–10
- Fails to grant full access to resources consultant needs to do assignment
- Does not use consultant effectively due to a lack of organizational policy on hiring outside services
- Unable to be both cooperative and the final decision maker (Haslett 1971; Jay 1977; Zaltman 1977)

Box 9.6.   Consultant Evaluation

A. *Consultant of Self*
  - Was the proposal well written and received?
  - Were the proposed tasks fully carried out?
  - Were the objectives of the assignment achieved?
  - Was a rapport with the client established from the beginning of the engagement? Was it established later?
  - Did the rapport help the consultant provide more effective services?
  - Did the consultant learn things from the engagement, the client, or the client group?
  - Have the consultant's capabilities improved during the assignment in a way that will be apparent in the next engagement?
  - Was the assignment completed on time and within budget?
  - Was a professional climate based on competence, objectivity, and integrity maintained throughout?
  - Were all stages of the consulting process fully carried out?
  - What techniques were used in each process stage, what were their results, and what could have been done to improve them?
  - Did the final report adequately reflect the work that was done and the lessons and insights that were gained?
  - Would the consultant and consultant team wish to work for the client again?

B. *Consultant of Client*
  - Did the client have an adequate understanding of the issue before the consultant arrived? Was it achieved during the course of the consultation?
  - Did the client change and make changes?
  - Is the client effectively implementing the recommended changes?
  - Will the client be able to carry on without the consultant?
  - Is the client examining other issues in the organization as a consequence of this assignment?
  - Did client communication channels enlarge and improve?
  - Did the consultant deal with client resistances to change and resolve conflicts?
  - Will the client ask the consultant to give assistance in the future (Steele 1975; Fuchs 1975; Shay 1974)?

the consultation. Some kind of written record of the dialogue session or sessions is advisable for use in later assignments. Also, these notes, comments, and ideas can be brought to the joint meeting of consultant and client, which is the final step in the evaluation process.

Client Evaluation

Using procedures similar to the consultant evaluation, the client comes to grips with the questions in box 9.7 to find ways to improve communications with consultants and other members of the organization.

Joint Evaluation

Upon completion of the separate client and consultant evaluation, both parties meet to assess each other's performance (Merry 1977). The ground rules are based on the client-consultant relationship to date. The more open the relationship and the greater the achievement of the consulting objectives, the deeper and more honest the respective evaluations are likely to be. The client, in general, is interested in airing his frank feelings about the consulting process, relationship, and results. The client also wants to determine whether the consultant services should be retained in the future. The consultant is interested in obtaining feedback from the client and, depending upon its tone, in negotiating conditions under which further assignments would be done.

The meeting consists of the consultant and consultant team, and the client and client team. It might also be advisable to have a third party—someone whom both client and consultant know and respect—present just to listen to and, if necessary, arbitrate or mediate any communication between them. This does not mean that the joint session is for conflict resolution; rather it is for airing perspectives. The selected place should be "neutral territory," to reflect both parties' intentions of fairness. Each party presents its evaluation, after which it is discussed by both groups. Eventually, a clear understanding is reached on the actions and feelings of both parties throughout the consulting experience.

This session is a high-risk one for both client and consultant. It is so for the consultant if, for instance, he had presented what he considered to be a dynamic, achievement-oriented image, and client feedback does not support this. It may be a high-risk situation for the client if his real motivations differ from those that were expressed at the outset of the assignment, either because of personal or organizational reasons. If the genuine motivations are revealed for the first time in this session, it will undermine the client's credibility with the consultant, and possibly

Box 9.7. Client Evaluation

A. *Client of Self*
- Was there a firm commitment to change?
- Was every effort made to define and understand the issue before calling in a consultant?
- Was a rapport well established between client and consultant by the end of the engagement?
- Has the rationale for using a consultant been justified?
- Did the client work well with the client team?
- What was learned from this experience? What are its likely effects on client management responsibilities?
- What kind of approach to organizational issues is likely to be taken in the future?
- Has the consulting assignment benefited both the client group and the entire organization?

B. *Client of Consultant*
- Could the consultant have utilized a more effective procedure?
- How did the consultant incorporate changes in the client concerns during the course of the engagement?
- Are the preliminary results positive and reflective of the client's expectations?
- Are the consultant recommendations the right ones, and should they be fully implemented?
- Were the expenditures of time and money reasonable and needed?
- Did the consultant provide the agreed-upon services stated in the contract?
- Did the final report adequately reflect and describe the extent of the consulting engagement?
- Should the consultant be retained or called in for future work?

jeopardize the entire results of the consultation. Even so, the underlying feelings and viewpoints of both will hopefully emerge so that pragmatic considerations can be addressed. If the evaluation discloses that the objectives of the consultation have not been met, further work might be needed. It may also become apparent that the time is not right for fully implementing the resolution pathway, or that a different consultant is needed to proceed further with the issue. In any case, the consultant will make reasonable efforts to accommodate the current client situation in an honest and professional manner.

Box 9.8 is a form that provides guidelines to the interactive evaluation. The form is to be filled in by consultant and client before the meeting and

Box 9.8.   Joint Evaluation

A. To be completed by client and consultant before meeting:
   - What are the major gains made by this assignment?
   - What are the major drawbacks incurred by this assignment?
   - What improvements can still be made?
   - Overall evaluation of consultant.
   - Overall evaluation of client.

B. At the meeting:

   - Remaining considerations for discussion
       Points   *Possible Actions*
   - Points raised by other party during presentation
       Points   *Possible Actions*
   - Potential for future client/consultant engagement
       Potential—Pro and Con   *Reasons*

used as a catalyst for further discussion during the meeting. If the client is first to share his evaluation and impressions, then the consultant reacts and responds initially. In like manner, the consultant presents his evaluation and the client responds. Thereafter, mutual discussion ensues on particular points still remaining in the contract, ways in which the client can continue the changes begun in the engagement, and possibilities for follow-up engagement.

Once both groups have weighed the positive attributes and negative outcomes of the consulting engagement, then future endeavors can be discussed in the more secure and trusting environment created by this mutual self-disclosure (Egerton 1970). First, has the issue been brought to a point where the client and client group can monitor the changes and implement additional required changes? If the answer is no, then it may still be necessary to retain the consultant for a variety of reasons—because his services are important and still needed, because bringing in someone else could mean high start-up costs, and because his familiar presence is already acceptable to organization personnel. On the other hand, the client should be wary of creating an unhealthy dependence on the consultant that could lead to unjustified costs or that might eventually cloud the consultant's objectivity and reduce his ability to produce useful and successful results.

If consultation is still needed, but not on a full-time basis, one option is for the consultant to come in for periodic scrutiny of the client's situation. The consultant might come in every two to three months to reassess the client's changed conditions. If there are any "bugs" to be worked out, these can probably be dealt with during the short consulting visits or delegated to others in the organization. Then, if new issues arise or old issue resolutions begin to show negative consequences, the consultant is available for direct, short-term analysis and suggestions on how to cope with these new conditions.

VALIDITY OF EVALUATION PROCEDURES

An evaluation of the consulting engagement is generally done for three reasons:

1. To become fully aware of the shortcomings of the assignments
2. To appreciate the value of the contributions made by the assignment
3. To understand how future engagements could be improved

That is fine as far as it goes, but to effectively make use of the time and effort expended in evaluating the performance of consultant and client, the evaluation must be incorporated into the client's organizational environment. This task is one of the last major change efforts of the assignment. It can be the most important in the long run.

Over the last few years, studies have been conducted exploring the merits of consulting assignments in various organizational situations. A survey of social work consultants found that most agencies using consulting services were ambivalent about the idea of consultation. The consultants found many clients ill prepared for the consultation, while the client organizations showed a lack of planning commitment to the effort. Most agencies did not have policies regarding the use of consultants. Many consultants sensed resistances of various types by the clients to the consultation (Kadushin 1978). On the technical side, the effects of consulting using an Operations Research formulation in the solution of urban problems were also analyzed. It was discovered that few of the clients saw any real benefits arising from the consultation to the client group, larger organization, or the public (Brewer 1973).

How can the consulting assignment be a positive and productive experience for the client? First, the process of consulting needs to be understood by the client and oriented to his organization. Questionnaires received from 172 small manufacturers in Virginia showed that the more satisfied clients tended to

- Have multiple experiences with consultants
- Restrict assignments—usually to a specific department
- Avoid using consultants for broad, complex problems

- Have multiple reasons for needing consultant assistance
- Engage in preliminary analysis of the issue
- Consider two or more consultant candidates
- Obtain written proposals and cost estimates
- Use the consultant's reputation as a significant factor in consultant selection
- Provide extensive communication for client staff
- Be cooperative in working with the consultant, but also establish controls and evaluation procedures
- Be willing to accept and implement recommendations (Ekey 1964)

Also, the client with a positive perspective toward change tended to be more satisfied with the results of the engagement. Twenty-five organizations involved in some kind of change were examined for successful consultations. Those organizations that had positive consulting experiences were characterized as being capable of adjusting to change. The consultants employed by these organizations were competitively chosen, had the necessary training and experience, and showed interest in and commitment to the change effort (Franklin 1976).

William Dunn (1977), a noted behavioral scientist, extended this characterization in a study of 67 reports of organization change efforts. He found that the successful consulting engagement was one in which the client and consultant had established a collaborative relationship, the consultant had adopted a participative orientation rather than the role of expert, and the client and client group exerted a high level of participation in all phases of consulting, particularly decision making and evaluation. Leonard Goodstein, a respected social psychologist, added that "the strongest evidence on the effectiveness of consultation is . . . the institutionalization of change. . . . The client system and the consultant need patience and perseverance in order for the change process to occur and be institutionalized" (Goodstein 1978, 158–161).

How can the consulting assignment be a positive and productive experience for the consultant in the long run? There are two elements that are necessary to accomplish this.

First, it is necessary to mark or celebrate the completion of the contract in some way (G. Lippett 1978). A closing "ceremony" defines the boundaries of the accomplishments and scuttles the sense of unfinished business that can result if the assignment is permitted to drift to an indefinite end. At the same time, provisions must be made for any extra assistance that will be required beyond the completion of the assignment.

The second element is reflected in the internal use of insights gained from the assignment within the consulting group. Discussions with consulting team members about ways in which the consulting organization can benefit from this assignment and the incorporation of the resulting insights into their working knowledge are needed to accomplish this. The following questions could be asked to stimulate this process:

What elements of the consultant organization need modification?
What new procedures should be used in any or all stages of consulting?
What interpersonal factors were brought out in the assignment that require attention?
What were the best moments of the assignment? Why?
What were the worst moments of the assignment? Why?
What has the consultant organization learned from this assignment?

Some or all of these questions may have been answered in the consultant evaluation described earlier. In either case, the emphasis here is on enlarging the ability of the consulting unit to deal with future client situations. In summary, as Swartz and Lippitt have remarked, "There is no one right way to evaluate. Consultants and clients need to invent evaluation systems appropriate to their needs and based on proven principles of evaluation" (Swartz 1979, 233). Such "principles" have been articulated throughout this chapter.

Case Example 9.1. Is a Joint Evaluation Worth It?

Barbara James, the principal of Land Options, Inc., a management consulting firm, was called to do a management audit of a large real estate corporation named Property Max. It appeared the corporation had made a series of miscalculations in buying and selling commercial properties. James and her staff did the management audit and discovered the following:

- In each case where a loss occurred, the seller needed to sell the property to raise cash due to a poor financial position.
- In each case where less commission was made than originally assumed, the buyer and seller talked more between themselves making minimum use of the realty executive.
- In each case where low income occurred, the property sold had been listed at its assessed value, generally five or more years out of date.

James met with the chief executive officer of Property Max, Jack Swartz, to discuss the findings. James said she would have the final report to Swartz within two weeks with suggestions on how to improve operations.

The first suggestion she made was for James's staff and Swartz's staff to each do an evaluation of how well the consulting assignment was done.

Next, after each side had reviewed their own performance, James suggested coming together for a mutual review of the consulting engagement.

Swartz was taken aback at first, but the more he considered these suggestions, the stronger he felt about doing an evaluation. After all, he reasoned, here is a chance for us to find out how good my staff is and soundly determine whether James really helped us. Each side completed an evaluation procedure separately. Then James briefed Swartz on the procedure to be followed in the joint session. James met with Swartz and the senior management team.

In the course of discussions, three additional management areas were recognized as "weak spots" in the corporation's operations:

1. Unused planning
2. Need for more motivation of new employees
3. Lack of career paths for present employees

Interestingly enough, James and Swartz had independently uncovered these concerns during their separate evaluations. Thus, these insights led to a follow-on management consulting contract.

REVIEW AND EXTENSION

This chapter has described the last stage of the consulting process—namely, the writing of the final report and the evaluation of the consulting effort. Both of these give client and consultant differing means to reflect on the assignment and the potential for future consulting services. The report provides the client with a synopsis of the entire engagement, including the results obtained. It also provides an opportunity for the consultant to articulate the essentials of the consulting process through the resolution of the client's issue. The evaluation requires joint collaboration and allows the consulting process to be examined and completed. The sense of closure this conveys is an important factor in client and consultant satisfaction with the completed assignment.

The client's attitude at the end of the consulting engagement can run the gamut from frustration and disappointment to confidence and satisfaction. Whatever opinion the client has at the end of the assignment is the culmination of all that preceded it, not just a passing mood. The evaluation efforts at the end of the consultation are designed to cue the client into the reasons behind his feelings. The evaluation should also serve to complete the implied objective of the consultant—namely, to instill within the client a greater sense of independence and security in the handling of his own issues.

Clients or consultants may shy away from a final evaluation for a variety of reasons. A consultant may hesitate to ask for definitive feedback if he is concerned about getting another contract from the organization. A client that is under pressure to produce may develop a win-lose attitude that can be transferred to the consultant. Problems that normally arise during the course of the consulting assignment can lose proportion and be translated into anxieties about consultant competency. These can be magnified into fears about how the consultant's performance will reflect on the client's status and potential for advancement within the organization, and might lead him to restrict any post-contract dialogue with the consultant or consultant team. The final evaluation serves a valuable function in the consulting process, and it is the task of the consultant to encourage it so that both consultant and client can benefit from it.

Chapter 10

Retrospect and Prospect

OVERVIEW

Consulting results in organizational change through the interaction of client and consultant. When the assignment is successful, the change is smoothly incorporated into the day-to-day business of the client organization, and client and consultant part company, pleased with their mutual accomplishment. But few assignments end as unqualified successes. When, in spite of all efforts, the resolution of the issue is less than optimal, does the consultant simply shrug his shoulders and hope for better luck next time? Or, is there still something to be learned from the experience, some way to isolate the reasons for the complete or partial failure of an assignment and to improve its outcome or at least carry this hard-won knowledge on to the next assignment? Often, a predisposition to failure is built into the consulting process by conflicting personal goals and by the very nature of the interaction. The result is too often an unsatisfactory outcome that is accepted by both client and consultant, from which no one benefits. By working with the known pitfalls of the process, these formerly negative factors can be used constructively to forge a new bond between consultant and client to avoid the development of such a no-win situation. This chapter brings together the attitude of change with the practices of change. The "new consulting" that will emerge from enhanced client-consultant interaction is explored, along with its ramifications for the consulting process and for the professional growth of consulting.

CONSULTING AND FAILURE: A BROAD VIEW

When an issue is examined in the framework of the consulting process, certain assumptions and value judgments are made that form the theoretical basis for the consultant's future actions. The stage is set for problems that can ultimately lead to failure when a disparity between theory and practice emerges. If a consultant does not recognize when the facts of a specific situation no longer fit a general theory, or does not notice that his client has made a different set of assumptions and value judgments, then the gap widens and the likelihood of failure increases. As two noted organizational psychologists, David Kolb and Alan Frohman, state, "The failure condition is far more common in consulting than is generally recognized and is extremely embarrassing for both the consultant and the client. . . . The mutual face-saving efforts that result often preclude using the experience as a learning situation for either the consultant or the client" (Kolb 1970, 64).

The problems that have arisen within the two major strains of consulting, Operations Research (OR) and Organization Development (OD), illustrate the limitations that can accompany the consulting process.

I. Operations Research

As has been stated, OR is a relative latecomer to the study of management. It grew out of the scientific management principles of the 1930s. By the 1960s, its theory and techniques were widely accepted (if less widely practiced) by the academic and professional communities. Yet, OR was not evolving quickly enough to reflect the changing nature of the issues that were facing clients. OR was originally used by upper management to formulate policy. As the success rate of OR assignments declined, top managers grew reluctant to use OR techniques. Instead, OR became relegated to technical staffs, who used it for solving specific engineering or economic problems. Today, OR practitioners are more involved with the structure rather than the content of issues.

Thus, OR has come to be identified with the use of mathematical models and algorithms rather than the ability to carry out the consulting process.

What prompted this change in OR application and use? As Russell Ackoff, one of the founders of OR, describes it, OR's "method is analytic and its models are of closed mechanical systems, not open purposeful ones" (Ackoff 1979a, 97). A system is a set of parts with relationships which constitute a whole. An analytic method is one in which a system is broken down into its component parts and in which these parts are made up of elemental units. Understanding comes from knowing how the parts work and being able to assemble them into a whole system. A model is mimicry of reality—an approximation and simplification of a "live" situation. Thus, the usefulness of models as analytical tools stems from the reduction of the target systems to their parts and the exclusion of the environment from the activity (Ackoff 1979a, 1979b).

There are other, open-ended types of systems that do not exclude environmental factors. A purposeful system is one which remains whole and retains its essential properties.

The system is understood as an *element* of a larger system. Although knowledge of the larger system is sought, such wisdom can never be fully attained; it can only be approached. The properties of the system include the *function* of the system in the larger system, the *intent* of the larger system, and the *purpose* of the system. Consideration of these properties necessitates an understanding of how such systems interact with their environment.

Therefore, models that represent such open-ended systems must

- Integrate changes in the larger and base systems
- Adapt to changes in the environment
- Respond to changes in the system
- Show interactions with the system's components

What has emerged from the evolution of OR is project management. Today, more and more consulting effort is done in a discrete time frame with better-defined objectives and the ability to more effectively monitor the emergence of the agreed-to solution and its implementation. In fact, managing a "portfolio" of such efforts is also becoming the norm. The key challenge is doing a stronger merger of technical resolution with personal interaction and development.

II. Organization Development

Like OR, OD grew out of the behavioral management principles of the 1930s. By the 1960s, the principles and practices of OD were found in a large number of organizations. Soon, "almost any activity concerned with development that took place within the organization automatically came to mean O.D." (Blake 1979, 13).

Yet, OD consulting assignments actually tend to be "either short term, crisis-oriented activities or low priority undertakings which ebb and flow with the economic and emotional conditions of the organization" (Alderfer 1977). The content of the OD technique is usually stressed, often to the exclusion of the changes in group interaction and personal behavior that are also required to resolve an organizational issue.

Further, many OD techniques are nonadaptive; that is, they are not designed to change with the shifting circumstances of organizations. Many OD programs are doomed to failure from the beginning for the following reasons:

- The lack of proper matching between OD effort and organizational needs
- The client assumption that OD will be the panacea for his organizational problems
- The static organizational perspective several OD techniques assume (Frohman 1976)

A deeper cause for continued failure in OD assignments is the tendency to ignore or rationalize failure. The responsibility for dealing with unsuccessful intervention lies with both the consultant and client. The consultant's concerns are three: reputation, client expectations, and consulting results. The consultant is working ostensibly to uphold and enlarge his reputation. This means generating a series of assignments that will lead to more engagements with greater compensation, responsibility, and influence. The client becomes aware of this budding reputation and in turn has greater expectations of the OD consultant. To provide more stimulating results, the consultant must take larger risks to resolve the issue through using a larger, broader, or more unique array of organizational techniques. When less-than-perfect outcomes occur, the client is disappointed. When unsatisfactory results occur, the consultant is quick to rationalize them, deny them, or, worse, blame someone else for their occurrence. Reassuring the client of the statistical validity of such results becomes the order of the day, rather than acknowledging and investigating the possible shortcomings of the results. The consultant then moves on to the next assignment. In this way, the cycle of deception repeats itself and becomes entrenched, starting a process of rationalization that reduces the chances for solid and honest results in the future (Mirvis 1977). The client reinforces this failure syndrome by reiterating the attitude of the consultant.

Pressures of time, scarce resources, and accountability force the client to cover up rather than try to learn from poorly done consulting engagements. The same personal factors that influence the consultant also affect the client, such as a need for visibility and prestige.

These factors may blind the client to discrepancies or possible problems with the outcome of the assignment. Since he hopes that errors will not be found, he may not look too closely for them. The likely outcome in this situation is that the results will be distorted to fit the client's need to save face. Once this pattern is established, no real learning will occur from the facets of the consulting assignment which did not go well.

What are the structural problems in OD that create and perpetuate this failure attitude? One of the basic shortcomings is that OD does not consider the complete organization, "the total system existing within a larger external environment which consists of interacting parts, including traditions, precedents, and past practices, all of which are geared, or should be toward achieving an overriding purpose" (Blake 1979, 16). Also the static nature of its method makes it ill suited to cope with the dynamics of change and its implementation. Third, OD consultants suffer from much the same organizational problems they seek to ameliorate in client systems. Why? Because "the profession of O.D. is still groping for its identity and for the characteristics and standards that will define it" (Alderfer 1977, 106).

Neither OR nor OD, then, has been flawless in its execution. Nor have practitioners of either school learned from the shortcomings of the system how to prevent future failures.

The systems orientation is so pervasive that the assignment is seen first as an opportunity to test a theory, experiment with a model, or use a set of techniques in some unique way. With this perspective, mistakes in the content of the assignment are viewed as aberrations of the system rather than as growth opportunities. In reaction to this, a service-oriented attitude has arisen in which the primary consulting motivation is to serve and fulfill the client's needs (Green 1977). The effectiveness of this result-oriented approach has been confirmed in many studies. One in particular determined the level of effectiveness of 14 operational research project groups that functioned in a billion-dollar, diversified corporation. Each project team consisted of OR analysts, representatives from the user groups, and representatives from the management information unit in the organization. It was concluded that the effective project groups directed a higher average number of internal communication hours toward user representatives than did the less effective groups. This result, in turn, stimulated high feelings of trust and cooperation (Amspoker 1973).

These results indicate that many consultants need to rethink their basic approach to the client. How can the consultant gain a fresh perspective on the issues the client faces daily? How can the failure syndrome work as a catalyst for constructive change in the consulting process? And what are the implications of these changes for both the client and consultant organizations?

III. Change

Change is the ability to alter one's circumstances. Change can be used to substitute a quantity for a reciprocal quantity, modify one's situation slightly, reverse one's position, or transform or convert something suddenly or gradually.

The concept of change is broad and open to many interpretations. Yet, there is a common thread that runs through all the definitions—that change is *the act of making a difference.*

This impetus to make something different receives predictable responses of resistance, anxiety, or fear from both those making the changes and those who will be directly affected by them. Such responses can impair the effective implementation of the required changes by blocking the change instigator's sensitivity to the total needs of those affected. Since the perpetrator assumes that he must be in control of the change effort, expressing his expectations and anxieties to those affected by the change is presumed to be out of the question. Instead, communication between consultant and client is narrowly focused on task accomplishment. The consequences of this type of communication are obvious—the changes will be difficult to implement and will meet with significant resistance.

Why are some clients more amenable to change than others? Certain characteristics have been found to be associated with a greater acceptance of change and with a more successful management style. These attributes are shown in table 10.1. All managers display behavior relating to the six characteristics of table 10.1. The manager who achieves, innovates, and directly assists in organizational growth, however, has made change an integral part of his management style and practices.

Table 10.1.   Characteristics for Change in an Organizational Environment

Less Successful Managers	Characteristics	More Successful Managers
Toward status quo	Orientation	Toward change
Concern for order, regularity, and security	Work philosophy	Concern for achievement, satisfaction, and willing to take risks
Directed to doing things "one best way"	Work philosophy	Open to more than one course of action
Procedure oriented		Results oriented
Based on successful experience with past techniques	Decision making	Based on evaluation of the situation, its data, and well-matched decision technique
Directed and unequal	Relationships	Interactive and equal
View tasks and people separately	Leadership	View tasks and people together
Higher prestige, status, and monetary rewards	Aspirations	Greater personal growth, organization fulfillment, and successful responses to changing conditions

IV. Learning

The learning process occurs when one finds out more about the skills, customs, knowledge, and values of the society in which one lives. In an organization, learning occurs through the acquisition of information, which is then examined, evaluated, and acted upon. Such action precipitates a further need for more information.

Organizations need feedback from constituents and members about how well they are functioning. When the feedback is positive, the organization is functioning well. Such feedback serves to reinforce current organizational activities with only slight modifications to present policies and practices. The emphasis is on improvement of the existing system.

When the feedback is negative, there are fundamental aspects of the organization or its activities that are not functioning well (Mirvis 1977). Unlike the minor changes associated with positive feedback, tasks to reorganize or rework the goals of an organization are required to resolve the issues raised by negative feedback. In either instance the job of the consultant is to assist in setting up the feedback system, work with the client to set up a means of evaluating the feedback, and suggest improvements to the feedback process so that it can continue to be a growth opportunity for the client and his organization.

V. Synthesis

The subject is consulting. The medium is change. The tool is learning.

The art form created is a responsive, adaptive, and holistic presentation of consulting. Its beauty lies in its duality: it has general contours that can be adapted to organizations of varying size and different goals (profit, public good or service). It can be used to address a wide range of issues in different cultural settings. Yet, it is also unique and distinctive in its ability to be tailored and fitted to the particular needs of an individual consulting engagement (Blake 1979). This is illustrated in table 10.2, which postulates a consulting picture in which the end results are equal in importance to the ways chosen for achieving them.

For the consultant, this new emphasis requires a release of previous hindrances that blocked the exploration of more meaningful pathways for client involvement. Specifically, it means viewing the attempt to change as having an intrinsic value equal to the result of the change. If the endeavor does not meet the client expectations, contract objectives, or organizational goals, then a new form of project accountability is to be employed. Instead of blaming each other for errors and the failure of the consultation, clients and consultants can feel free to share their respective mistakes mindful that the lessons learned from this sharing can help the

Table 10.2.   Integration of Consulting Process with Consulting Style

Consulting Process	Consulting Style
Issue Recognition	Roles and responsibilities
Consultant Selection	Proposal development
Engagement Beginning	Client-consultant relationship
Issue Definition	Conducting an interview
Resolution Pathways	Giving and receiving feedback
Pathway Implementation	Directing a meeting
Monitoring and Termination	Overcoming resistance to change
Evaluation and Follow-Up	Conflict resolution
	Modifications to consulting organizations

change effort. "No-fault" change places no burden of guilt on anyone. It reinforces the idea that failure in consulting can be turned into potential for future success by sharing the learning that is going on throughout the consulting experience (McGill 1976). Further, through such recognition, the client learns not merely to react to issues in a crisis manner, but to move toward early anticipation of possible issues so that they can be defused at an early stage.

Anticipation describes a state of preparedness rather than anxiety. The preparation includes

- A readiness to perceive hard and soft data
- The confidence to cope with personalities and personal resistance
- The assurance that the best possible solution has been reached

That is, client and consultant together will grow from the consulting assignment because both want to. Table 10.2 is a model, but a model that portrays the process's procedures, dynamics, and techniques in a closer approximation of the current and future consulting reality than its scientific management or behavioral management predecessors. The consulting of tomorrow will be "a complex educational strategy intended to change the beliefs, attitudes, values, and structures of organizations so they can better adapt to new technologies, markets, challenges, and the dizzying rate of change itself" (Bennis 1969, 261).

VI. Educational Strategy

Consulting differs from most established professions in its paucity of formal communication channels. The lack of uniform licensing procedures, inter-professional conferences, comprehensive educational programs, and a distinct research activity has hampered the evolution of consulting as a field. Not enough practitioners conceive of their work as creating and transmitting knowledge to fellow professionals and clients. Further, most of the training of consultants takes place outside direct degree-granting university programs. That is, other academic areas substitute for consulting education. Innovations are usually communicated more by practice than education, which makes systematic, formal evolutions of new techniques difficult. Finally, the disparate nature of training courses causes difficulty in specifying exactly what a competent professional should know.

The solutions to the above problems in consultant education can be found in three areas: the school, the firm, and the association.

There are few courses devoted to consulting per se. A course which seeks to integrate the scientific/engineering aspects of consulting with the behavioral/psychological facets is rare indeed. There are, however, some attempts at fostering a learning environment where participation is considered as important as results. In these schools, students struggle with the tension between disciplinary courses and interdisciplinary education, and evaluation is not based solely on the accumulation of knowledge, but also on the effective and creative application of new resolutions to organizational issues (Ackoff 1979a).

One result of increased university training in consulting would be a greater interest in consulting research and evaluation. Research efforts would focus on interdisciplinary projects using social science and engineering methods. These projects could examine various elements of any of the stages of the consulting process or facets of the consulting style. In addition, evaluation would evolve as a related but separate subject with its own tools for assessing the short, intermediate, and longer-term impacts of the consulting assignment on the organization, client, and issue, respectively. The hope is that the output of such research and evaluation endeavors could be fed back to the consulting practitioners and forward to prospective clients (G. Lippett 1979).

A second area where major improvements could be made in the professionalism of consulting is within the consulting firm. Professional education is a prerequisite for advancement. Such education seeks to impart not only the "stuff" of consulting but also the "art" of being a practitioner. Courses taken throughout one's career provide new challenges and pave the way to mature understanding of the client-consultant interaction.

A sequence of training seminars would allow the consultant to understand and measure career growth in terms of human growth, as shown in table 10.2. This diagram represents the paradigm through which the consultant is able to integrate theory and experience, insight and application, and personal and vocational characteristics in an emerging sense of professional maturity.

A third way to combat the lack of educational opportunities in consulting is through the professional society or association. These organizations have traditionally been organized by discipline. Thus, consultants have been grouped by the profession for which they are consulting, rather than with other consultants in various disciplines. It is time to follow the lead of the engineering societies in having the major consulting associations combine efforts for education, promotion, and meetings. In this way, the consultant will be able to benefit from the synergistic knowledge and experience of the various professional organizations whose members do consulting. Also, such interaction could serve to reinforce the common elements in consulting, opening new areas for research, practice, and teaching.

To reiterate, consulting is still viewed as one of those vocational activities that is often practiced and rarely learned. Bringing together the academic preparation, continuing education in a work environment, and combined resources of interdisciplinary associations can lead to new channels for information flow, new sources for professional development, and new organizations for future, higher-quality practice.

Case Example 10.1. To Change or Not to Change: Is That the Question?

Background: For the sake of discussion, let us assume that there are two types of personalities. One is type D for *directed*; the other is type P for *participative*. Type D is punctual and self-reliant. Type P is interactive and group oriented. Type D is task directed and likes to know how things work. Type P likes to know more about people and people who want to know. Type D thrives on achievement, results, and product; that is, D is output oriented. Type P desires understanding, insight, and satisfaction in activities undertaken; that is, P is input oriented. For Type D, the world is a challenge, the individual a master. For Type P, the world is a mystery, the individual an explorer. Type D people seem to enclose themselves with type P people. Type P people seem to expand themselves by interacting with type D people.

Dialogue: At a seminar on the future of the organization, Diane Strong and Pauline Quest happened to sit next to each other. During the coffee break, they struck up a conversation and decided to have lunch together. Over coffee, the talk centered on their job interests. Diane described how she moved into her current position in the business organization: "As I grew up, I was told that there are only two things worth having: your freedom and your will to do something with it. Well, living in this country I never much worried about freedom, so I concentrated on making something of myself. I knew that business meant accomplishing ends efficiently and productively. That is, from each action day by day, and each plan year by year, to increase profits, sales, and business activities. For me, a strong arm of leadership is the answer. Organizing and controlling the resources—money, goods, and people—in a steadfastly directed manner is what produces results. And my company has produced results— plenty of them. We've boosted profits every year, created many new jobs, and influenced the economy of our industry to an ever-increasing degree. Not bad for 20 years worth of hard labor, don't you think?"

Pauline responded by saying, "Let me understand you. This drive of yours was to show more each year; that is, that whatever means were used, within reason, they justified the end. How are conditions now?"

Diane admitted, "They could be better. Our markets seem to be sluggish, our employees lethargic, and our equipment in need of repair."

"Do you think that somewhere along the way your vision has gotten clouded?" Pauline asked.

"Yes," answered Diane. This admission precipitated the following discussion:

P: What have you done to cope with the present conditions in your company?

D: Oh, we've tried all sorts of stimulants to get these folks back on track.

P: What kinds of stimulants?

D: Job incentive programs, group production activities, management advancement schemes, and so on. Nice techniques—if they work.

P: I take it these "schemes" have not shown much positive results. Correct?

D: Ah, yes, that's about right.

P: What then are the underlying causes of the modified conditions in your company?

D: People don't seem to want our products.

P: That's the bottom line.

D: More or less.

P: Have you considered that quite possibly the bottom line is found directly inside your company? From what you say, it seems that the issue is not the sales themselves but how the sales are made. In other words, your strict concern with the end blocked a sensitivity toward the means.

D: What are you saying?

P: I'm saying that it is time to do some soul-searching about the fundamentals—why your company is in existence, what good your products have given to society, and what the employees' present dissatisfactions are. It seems that you need to make some basic decisions about what kind of a future organization you want rather than just a vague direction.

D: What are you saying about my role?

P: First off, I feel you don't have a role. Being successful and being one of the main forces in a company are not facets of a role; instead, they are basic manifestations of your lifestyle. Second, the operations, procedures, communication, rewards, policies, goals, and products are all lumped together. That is, I sense the company goes through the same actions in dealing with an equipment failure as with a disappointing job performance, and so forth. What I'm suggesting is that you take a long and critical look at the ways you block internal influence from making a difference in the company.

D: Does this imply that we should scrap our product line, give up the company, and go fishing?

P: Nothing of the sort. The point is simple: your company needs to decide what it is today, where it's going, and how it wants to get there. These are decisions that you cannot make without the input of those working for you.

The waiter brought them the check. As they were leaving the restaurant, Diane said, "I don't know. It seems like a big risk. We could stand to lose a lot."

Pauline replied, "If you are willing to remain open to the concept of *change* and consciously work with it, the hard times could actually be exciting, and innovative. The challenge is up to you—all of you."

VII. Consulting: A Forward Look

What of consulting as it will be taught, practiced, and improved? The three nouns which focus this discussion are "extension," "interdependence," and "control." Table 10.2 lays the foundation for the new consulting. It is a synthesis of the state-of-the-art in thinking and using consultant services. The process is the sequence of steps necessary to complete a consulting assignment. As the elements of the consulting style proceed from left to right across the page, the skill level increases and the perceptions become more mature as they are applied to consulting engagements. For now, it is enough to say that many consulting practitioners need to *extend* their understanding and abilities through this model. As the process and style of consulting change, so would the interactions shown in table 10.2. In fact, the order from initiation to completion of consulting could well be different in the future. All elements in process and style are *interdependent* and subject to outside influences, which makes them inherently changeable. One cannot demonstrate the consulting style without the consulting process. But, by the same token, one cannot carry out the consulting process *without* perceptive application of the consulting style.

It is also true that consulting is not a discrete function performed in a unique way with onetime results. Consulting is the continuous transmittal of insights and recommendations about how the client organization can more effectively respond to changes from within and from without. This implies that when the consultant contract ends, the consulting process continues—by the client. The process is internalized and becomes the operating model for uncovering, defining, and resolving future organizational issues. The results of the consulting experience are used by the client management to heighten its awareness and understanding of the governance of the organization.

Shifting the consultant function to the client as the end of the assignment nears results in more effective control in the client environment. This control is manifested as a better use of organizational resources in an interactive manner. The planning of company structure and goal setting now become shared functions among members of the client staff.

Planning and direction become design activities requiring much participation. Evaluation of organizational performance and activities takes on new meaning as input is solicited from members of the client group. Thus, *control* for the participative organization does not mean restricting involvement in organization change. Rather, control means a greater diversity of ways to effectively respond to the changing organizational environment.

As a greater flexibility, openness, and concern for interaction are inculcated in clients through the examples of client and consultant colleagues, the nature of consulting will change. First, client facility with self-diagnosis and correction of issues will improve. This means consultants will be called in more to do specific but integrated consulting tasks and less to provide general assistance. Second, consultant firms need to be more internally responsive to changes in professional staff career needs. Greater in-house training will be required to keep abreast of client abilities and to learn new areas where consulting services are needed.

Third, client procedures for selecting consultants may change. Consultants need to be able to instigate as well as to respond to such changes. This implies that the successful consultant will be increasingly facile at integrating the style and process of consulting and will have greater freedom to do so.

References

Ackoff, Russell L. 1956. "The Development of Operational Research as a Science." *Operational Research*, June.

———. 1972. *Redesigning the Future*. New York: John Wiley & Sons.

———. 1979a. "The Future of Operational Research Is Past." *Journal of the Operational Research Society*, February: 93–104.

———. 1979b. "Resurrecting the Future of Operational Research." *Journal of the Operational Research Society*, March: 189–199.

———. 1999. *Ackoff's Best*. New York: John Wiley & Sons.

Ackoff, Russell L., and Sheldin Rovin. 2005. *Beating the System*. San Francisco: Berrett-Kohler.

Adams, James. 1976. *Conceptual Blockbusting*. San Francisco: San Francisco Book Company.

Alderfer, Clayton P., et al. 1977. "Organization Development: The Profession and the Practitioner." In Philip Mirvis et al., *Failures in Organization Development and Change*. New York: John Wiley & Sons.

AMA (American Management Association). 1977. *Focus: The AMA Guide to Business Development*. New York: AMA.

Amspoker, Robert D., et al. 1973. "Organizational Factors Related to Operations Research Project Group Effectiveness." In *Advancing, Applying and Teaching the Decision Sciences*. Atlanta: American Institute for Decision Sciences, 102–105.

Andreychuck, Theodore. 1964. "Psychology of Consulting." *Management Sciences*, March/April: 53–59.

Argyris, Chris. 1965. *Organizational Innovation*. Homewood, IL: Dorsey Press.

Association of Consulting Engineers of Canada (ACEC). 1976. *The Practice of Consulting Engineering*. Revised edition. Ottawa: ACEC.

Association of Consulting Management Engineers. 1972. "How to Control the Quality of a Management Consulting Engagement." New York: Business Consultants.

Axelrod, Richard H. 2000. *Terms of Engagement: Changing the Way We Change Organizations*. San Francisco: Berrett-Koehler.

Baird, Bruce F. 1978. *Introduction to Decision Analysis*. North Scituate, MA: Duxbury Press.

Baker, H. Kent, et al. 1976. "Diagnosis: Key to O.D. Effectiveness." *Personnel Journal*, October: 506–510.

Barnard, Chester I. 1938. *The Functions of the Executive*. Cambridge, MA: Harvard University Press.

Barnes, Ralph M. 1968. *Motion and Time Study*. New York: John Wiley & Sons.

Beary, Michael P., et al. 1979. "Government Report and Letter Writing." Special Programs, Graduate School, U.S. Department of Agriculture, October 1–15.

Bell, Chip R., and Leonard Nadler. 1979. *The Client-Consultant Handbook*. Houston: Gulf.

Bellman, Geoffrey M. 1990. *The Consultant's Calling: Bringing Who You Are to What You Do*. San Francisco: Jossey Bass Business and Management Series.

Bennis, Warren G. 1969. *Organization Development: Its Nature, Origin and Prospects*. Reading, MA: Addison-Wesley.

Bergen, Bernard J., et al. 1970. "Experts and Clients: The Problem of Structural Strain in Psychiatric Consultation." *Diseases of the Nervous System*, 31: 399.

Bermont, Hubert. 1979. *The Successful Consultant's Guide to Writing Proposals and Reports*. Washington, DC: Bermont Books.

———. 1981. *The Successful Consultant's Guide to Winning Government Contracts*. Washington, DC: Bermont Books.

Black, J. Stewart, and Hal B. Gregersen. 2002. *Leading Strategic Change*. Upper Saddle River, NJ: Financial Times Prentice-Hall.

Blake, Robert R., et al. 1979. "Why the O.D. Movement Is 'Stuck' and How to Break It Loose." *Training and Development Journal*, September: 12–20.

Block, Peter. 2000. *The Flawless Consulting Fieldbook and Companion: A Guide to Understanding Your Expertise*. San Francisco: Jossey Bass/Pfeiffer.

Bly, Robert. 1998. *Six-Figure Consultant*. Chicago: Upstart Publishing.

Brewer, G. D. 1973. *Politicians, Bureaucrats and the Consultant*. New York: Basic Books.

Briggs, K., et al. 1976. *Myer-Briggs Type Indication*. Palo Alto, CA: Consulting Psychologists Press.

Broekhuizen, Richard J. 1979. *Graphic Communications*. Bloomington, IL: McKnight.

Combs, A., et al. 1969. *Florida Studies in the Helping Professions*. Social Sciences Monograph No. 37. Gainesville: University of Florida Press.

Conner, Daryl R. 1992. *Managing at the Speed of Change*. New York: Villard Books.

Cope, Mick. 2005. *The Seven C's of Consulting: The Definitive Guide to the Consulting Process*. New York: Financial Times.

Crosby, Andrew C. 1968. *Creativity and Performance in Industrial Organization*. London: Tavistock Publications.

Culbert, Samuel A. 1974. *The Organization Trap and How to Get Out of It*. New York: Basic Books.

Dalton, Gene W. 1974. "Influence and Organization Change." In *Organizational Psychology: A Book of Readings*. Englewood Cliffs, NJ: Prentice-Hall, 401–425.

Davey, Neil G. 1971. *The External Consultant's Role in Organizational Change*. MSU Business Studies. East Lansing: Michigan State University Press.

Davidson, Robert L., III. 1990. *Contracting Your Services*. New York: John Wiley & Sons.

de Bono, Edward. 1973. *Think Tank*. Toronto: Think Tank Corp.

Dinkmeyer, Dan, et al. 1973. *Consulting, Facilitating Human Potential and Change Processes*. Columbus, OH: Charles E. Merrill.

Downs, Cal W., et al. 1977. *The Organizational Communicator*. New York: Harper & Row.

Doyle, Michael. 1976. *How to Make Meetings Work*. New York: Wyden Books.

Dunn, William N., et al. 1977. "Planned Organizational Change: Toward Grounded Theory." *Journal of Applied Behavioral Science*, 13: 135–138.

Egerton, Henry G., et al. 1970. "Consultants: Selection, Use, and Appraisal." National Industrial Conference Board, New York, *Report No. 13*.

Ekey, David C., et al. 1964. *The Use of Consultants by Manufacturers*. Bureau of Business Research. Richmond, VA: University of Richmond Press.

Elbing, Alvar. 1978. *Behavioral Decisions in Organizations*. Englewood Cliffs, NJ: Prentice-Hall.

Emerson, Harrington. 1913. *The Twelve Principles of Efficiency*. New York: Engineering Magazine Co.

Etzioni, Amitai. 1964. *Modern Organizations*. Englewood Cliffs, NJ: Prentice-Hall.

Fayol, Henri. 1949. *General and Industrial Management*. New York: Pitman.

Ferner, Jack D. 1980. *Successful Time Management*. New York: John Wiley & Sons.

Festinger, Leon. 1964. *Conflict, Decision, and Dissonance*. Stanford, CA: Stanford University Press.

Fisher, Norman. 1967. "How to Get the Most Out of Your Consultant." *Management Decision*, Spring: 60–62.

Flint, Jerry. 1979. "A New Breed—Professional Union Breakers." *Forbes*, June 25: 29–30.

Francis, Lee F. 1976. "Providing a Link to Foreign Countries." *Consulting Engineer*, March: 91–93.

Franklin, J. L. 1976. "Characteristics of Successful and Unsuccessful Organizational Development." *Applied Behavioral Science*, 12: 471–492.

Freedman, Rick. 2000. *The IT Consultant: A Commonsense Framework for Managing the Client Relationship*. San Francisco: Jossey Bass/Pfeiffer.

French, Wendell L., et al. 1978. *Organization Development*. Englewood Cliffs, NJ: Prentice-Hall.

Frohman, Mark A., et al. 1976. "Action Research as Applied to Organization Development." In *Organizational Effectiveness*, ed. S. Lee Spray. Kent, OH: Kent State University Press, 129–161.

Fuchs, Jerome H. 1975. *Making the Most of Management Consulting Services*. New York: AMACOM.

Garvin, Andrew P., and Hubert Bermont. 1980. *How to Win with Information or Lose without It*. Washington, DC: Bermont Books.

Gaskell, Philip. 1978. *From Writer to Reader*. Oxford: Clarendon Press.

Gauss, S. I., and C. M. Harris. 2001. *Encyclopaedia of Operations Research and Management Science*. Centennial Edition. Hingham, MA: Kluwer Academic.

George, Claude S., Jr. 1968. *The History of Management Thought*. Englewood Cliffs, NJ: Prentice-Hall.

Gibb, Jack. 1961. "Defensive Communication." *Journal of Communication*, September.

Glidewell, John C. 1959. "The Entry Problem in Consultation." *The Journal of Social Issues*, 15: 51–59.

Golightly, Henry O. 1964. "How to Select and Effectively Use a Management Consultant." *International Management*, November: 47–48.

Goodstein, Leonard D. 1978. *Consulting with Human Service Systems*. Reading, MA: Addison-Wesley.

Gordon, Gilbert, et al. 1978. *Quantitative Decision-Making for Business*. Englewood Cliffs, NJ: Prentice-Hall.

Gottfried, Ira S. 1969a. "Consulting Consultants." *Data Management*, June: 44–45.

———. 1969b. "Selecting a Consultant." *Journal of Data Management*, October: 32–35.

Green, Thad B. 1977. "How Do Your Quantitative Specialists Stack-Up?" *Business and Economic Perspectives*, Spring: 41–47.

———. 1978. *The Decision Science Process*. New York: Petrocelli Books.

Gunning, R. 1952. *The Technique of Clear Writing*. New York: McGraw-Hill.

Guttman, H. Peter. 1976. *The International Consultant*. New York: McGraw-Hill.

———. 1978. "International Arbitration: The Pros and Cons." *Consulting Engineer*, December: 68–70.

Hale, Judith A. 2007. *The Performance Consultant's Fieldbook: Tools and Techniques for Improving Organizations and People*. New York: John Wiley & Sons.

Haslett, J. W. 1971. "Decision Table for Engaging a Consultant." *Journal of Systems Management*, July: 12–14.

Herum, John. 1971. *Writing: Plans, Drafts and Revisions*. New York: Random House.

Hollander, Stanley C. 1963. *Business Consultants and Clients*. MSU Business Studies. East Lansing: Michigan State University Press.

Holtz, Herman. 1979. *Government Contracts, Proposalmanship and Winning Strategies*. New York: Plenum Press.

"How to Conduct a Post-Mortem on a Management Consultant." 1965. *Business Management*, December: 47–49.

Hoyt, Douglas B. 1997. *How to Start and Run a Successful Independent Consulting Business*. Lincolnwood, IL: NTC Business Books.

Hunt, Alfred. 1977. *The Management Consultant*. New York: John Wiley & Sons.

Huse, Edgar F. 1975. *Organizational Development and Change*. New York: West Publishing.

Jackson, Keith F. 1975. *The Art of Solving Problems*. New York: St. Martin's Press.

Jay, Anthony. 1977. "Rate Yourself as a Client." *Harvard Business Review*, July/August: 84–92.

Jung, Carl G. 1923. *Psychological Types*. London: Routledge and Kegan Paul.

Kadushin, Alfred. 1977. *Consultation in Social Work*. New York: Columbia University Press.

———. 1978. "Practice of Social Work Consultation: A Survey." *Social Work*, September: 372–379.

Kanter, Rosabeth Moss, Barry A. Stein, and Todd D. Jick. 1992. *The Challenge of Organizational Change*. New York: The Free Press.

Kilmann, Ralph H., et al. 1979. "Integrating the Benefits of Different Efforts at Management Consulting." In *The Academic Consultant Connection*, ed. George J. Gore et al. Dubuque, IA: Kendall/Hunt, 215–226.

Kindred, Alton B. 1973. *Data Systems and Management*. Englewood Cliffs, NJ: Prentice-Hall.

Kintler, David. 1997. *Streetwise Independent Consulting: Your Comprehensive Guide to Building Your Own Consulting Business*. Holbrook, MA: Adams Media Corporation.

Klein, Howard J. 1977. *Other People's Business*. New York: Mason/Charter.

Koehler, Jerry W., et al. 1976. *Organizational Communication, Behavioral Perspectives*. New York: Holt Rinehart & Winston.

Kolb, David A. 1970. "An Organization Development Approach to Consulting." *Sloan Management Review*, Fall.

———. 1974. "On the Dynamics of a Helping Relationship." In *Organizational Psychology: A Book of Readings*. Englewood Cliffs, NJ: Prentice-Hall, 371–379.

Kubr, M. 1976. *Management Consulting: A Guide to the Profession*. Geneva: International Labour Office.

Laing, R. D. 1972. *Politics of the Family and Other Essays*. New York: Vintage.

Lebell, Don. 1973. *The Professional Services Enterprise: Theory & Practice*. Sherman Oaks, CA: Los Angeles Publishing Co.

Leifer, Richard, et al. 1978. "Relationships of Personal Values with Group Process and Preferences for Organization and Structure." Amherst: University of Massachusetts, Department of Management.

Lesikar, Raymond V. 1977. *Report Writing for Business*. Homewood, IL: R.D. Irwin.

Levesque, Robert W. 1973. "How Not to Do Consulting." *Chemical Engineering*, June 11: 120–122.

Lewin, Marsha D. 1995. *The Overnight Consultant*. New York: John Wiley & Sons.

———. 1997. *The Consultants' Survival Guide*. New York: John Wiley & Sons.

Likert, Rensis. 1961. *New Patterns of Management*. New York: McGraw-Hill.

Lippitt, Gordon L. 1969. *Organizational Renewal*. New York: Appleton-Century Crofts.

———. 1972. "Criteria for Selecting, Evaluating and Developing Consultants." *Training and Development Journal*, August.

———. 1978. *The Consulting Process in Action*. La Jolla, CA: University Associates.

———. 1979. "Research in the Consulting Process." In *The Academic Consultant Connection*, ed. George J. Gore et al. Dubuque, IA: Kendall/Hunt, 159–167.

Lippitt, Ronald. 1959. "Dimensions of a Consultant's Job." *Journal of Social Issues*, 15, no. 2: 5–12.

Maister, David H. 2000. *True Professionalism: The Courage to Care about Your People, Your Clients, and Your Career*. New York: The Free Press

———. 2001. *The Trusted Advisor*. New York: Simon & Schuster.

Margulies, Newton. 1972. *Organizational Development, Values, Process, and Technology*. New York: McGraw-Hill.

———. 1978. *Conceptual Foundations of Organizational Development*. New York: McGraw-Hill.

Maynard, Harold B. 1952. *Industrial Engineering Handbook*. New York: McGraw-Hill.

Mayo, Elton. 1933. *The Human Problems of an Industrial Civilization*. Boston: Harvard Business School.

McFarland, Dalton E. 1958. "The Labor Relations Consultant as Contract Negotiator." *Personnel*, May/June: 44–51.

McGill, Michael E. 1976. "Assessing the Effectiveness of Organization Development Program." In *Organizational Effectiveness*, ed. S. Lee Spray. Kent, OH: Kent
State University Press, 123–128.

———. 1977. *Organizational Development for Operating Managers*. New York: AMA-
COM.

Merry, Uri, et al. 1977. *Developing Teams & Organizations: A Practical Handbook for
Managers and Consultants*. Reading, MA: Addison-Wesley.

Metzler, Ken. 1977. *Creative Interviewing*. Englewood Cliffs, NJ: Prentice-Hall.

Mial, A. Curtis. 1959. "What Is a Consultant?" *Public Relations Journal*, November:
31–34.

Michael, Donald N., et al. 1977. "Changing, Erring, and Learning." In *Failures in
Organization Development and Change*, ed. Philip H. Mirvis et al. New York: John
Wiley & Sons, 311–333.

Mintzberg, H. 1971. "Managerial Work: Analysis from Observation." *Management
Science*, October: B97–B110.

Mirvis, Philip H., et al., eds. 1977. "Failures in Organizational Development and
Change." In *Failures in Organization Development and Change*. New York: John
Wiley & Sons, 1–18.

Moorman, Thomas. 1979. *How to Work toward Agreement*. New York: Atheneum.

Morris, M. D. 1979. "Writing Professional and Technical Communications." Seminar given at George Washington University, Continuing Engineering Education Program, November 13–16.

Mundel, M. E. 1969. *Time and Motion Study*. Englewood Cliffs, NJ: Prentice-Hall.

Nelson, Bob, and Peter Economy. 1997. *Consulting for Dummies*. New York: Hun-
gry Minds.

Parkinson, C. Northcote. 1971. *The Law of Delay: Interviews and Outerviews*. Boston:
Houghton Mifflin.

Pattenaude, Richard L. 1979. "Consultants in the Public Sector." *Public Administration Review*, May/June.

Phillips, Jack. J. 2009. *The Consultant's Guide to Results-Driven Business Proposals:
How to Write Proposals That Forecast Impact and ROI*. New York: McGraw-Hill.

———. 2010. *The Consultant's Scorecard: Tracking Results and Bottom-Line Impact of
Consulting Projects*. 2nd edition. New York: McGraw-Hill.

Powers, Jacqueline K. 1999. *How to Start a Freelance Consulting Business*. New York:
Avon Books.

Pym, D. 1966. "Effective Management Performance in Organizational Change."
Journal of Management Studies, 3.

Rathbone, Robert R. 1966. *Communicating Technical Information*. Reading, MA:
Addison-Wesley.

Raybould, E. B., and A. L. Minter. 1971. *Problem Solving for Management*. London:
Institute of Work Study Practitioners.

Reddin, W. J. 1977. "Confessions of an Organizational Change Agent." *Training
and Development Journal*, October: 52–57.

Robbins, Paul R., et al. 1970. "Some Factors Influencing the Outcome of Consultation." *American Journal of Public Health*, 60: 524–534.

Rogers, Carl R. 1961. *On Becoming a Person*. Boston: Houghton Mifflin.

Rosenhead, Jonathan, and John Mingers, eds. 2001. *Rational Analysis for a Problematic World Revisited: Problem Structuring Methods for Complexity, Uncertainty and Conflict*. 2nd edition. Chichester, UK: John Wiley & Sons.

Ross, Valerie. 1977. "The Consultant as Lone Ranger." *Canadian Business*, September: 37.

Rowe, A. J. 1974. "The Myth of the Rational Decision-Maker." *International Management*, August: 38.

Schein, Edgar H. 1969. *Process Consultation: Its Role in Organizational Development*. Reading, MA: Addison-Wesley.

Schindler-Rainman, Eva, et al. 1975a. "The Consultant as Meeting Designer." *Journal of European Training*, Fall: 296–308.

———. 1975b. *Taking Your Meetings Out of the Doldrums*. Columbus, OH: The Association of Professional YMCA Directors.

Schroder, Marjan. 1974. "The Shadow Consultant." *Journal of Applied Behavioral Science*, 10, no. 4: 579–597.

Schwarz, Roger M. 2002. *The Skilled Facilitator: A Comprehensive Resource for Consultants, Facilitators, Managers, Trainers, and Coaches*. San Francisco: Jossey-Bass.

Schwartz, William L. K. 1958. "Using the Outside Expert." *Management Review*, August: 4

Seney, Wilson. 1963. *Effective Use of Business Consultants*. New York: Financial Executives Research Foundation.

Shay, Philip W. 1974. *How to Get the Best Results from Management Consultants*. New York: Association of Consulting Management Engineers.

Shenson, Howard L. 1980. *How to Strategically Negotiate the Consulting Contract*. Washington, DC: Bermont Books.

———. 1994. *Shenson on Consulting: Success Strategies from the Consultant's Consultant*. New York: John Wiley & Sons.

Silberman, Melvin L. 2001. *The Consultant's Toolkit: High-Impact Questionnaires, Activities and How-To Guides for Diagnosing and Solving Client Problems*. New York: McGraw-Hill.

———. 2003. *The Consultant's Big Book of Organization Development Tools: 50 Reproducible Intervention Tools to Help Solve Your Clients' Problems*. New York: McGraw-Hill.

Singsen, Antone G., III. 1980. "Meeting." *Legal Services Corporation News*, January/February: 2.

Skarke, Gary, Butch Holland, Bill Rogers, and Diane Landon. 1995. *The Change Management Toolkit: A Step-by-Step Methodology for Successfully Implementing Dramatic Organizational Change*. 2nd edition. Houston: WinHope Press.

Sommers, William P. 1973. "Management Consulting." In *The Creative Partnership: Government and the Professional Services*. Proceedings of the Fourth Users-Producers Conference. Washington, DC: National Bureau of Standards.

Steele, Fritz. 1975. *Consulting for Organizational Change*. Amherst: University of Massachusetts Press.

Swartz, Donald H., et al. 1979. "Evaluating the Consulting Process." In *The Client-Consultant Handbook*, ed. Chip R. Bell and Leonard Nadler. Houston: Gulf, 215–233.

Tatham, Laura E. 1964. *The Efficiency Experts*. London: Business Publications.

Taylor, Frederick W. 1947. *Scientific Management*. New York: Harper & Row.

Tepper, Ron. 1987. *The Consultant's Problem-Solving Workbook*. New York: Wiley-Interscience.

This, Leslie E. 1979. *The Small Meeting Planner*. Houston: Gulf.

Tilles, Seymour. 1961. "Understanding the Consultant's Role." *Harvard Business Review*, November/December: 87–99.

Turner, Rufus P. 1971. *Technical Report Writing*. San Francisco: Rinehart Press.

Van der Heijden, Kees, 1996. *Scenarios: The Art of Strategic Conversation*. Chichester, UK: John Wiley & Sons.

Van de Vliert, Evert. 1971. "The Organizational Consultant: Controller? Pilot? Coach?" *SAM Adv. Mgt. Jrnl.*, July: 19–26.

Walsh, John E. 1973. *Guidelines for Management Consultants in Asia*. Tokyo: Asian Productivity Organization.

Walton, Richard E. 1965. "Two Strategies of Social Change and Their Dilemmas." *Journal of Applied Behavioral Science*, April–June: 167–179.

Waterbow, Herbert Reed. 1970. "Management Consultants—Cure or Cancer in the Corporate Body?" *Paper Trade Journal*, January 26: 58–61.

Weil, Andrew Warren. 1978. "Tailor Graphics to Fit Presentations." *Consulting Engineer*, August: 36–38.

———. 1979. "Are You Preparing Too Many Proposals?" January: 40–43.

Wells, H. G. 1931. *Outline of History*. New York: Garden City Publishers.

Zallen, Harold, and Eugenia M. Zallen, 1976. *Ideas Plus Dollars, Research Methodology and Funding*. Norman, OK: Academic World Incorporated.

Zaltman, Gerald, et al. 1977. *Strategies for Planned Change*. New York: John Wiley & Sons.

Index

Breinigsville, PA USA
10 December 2010
250963BV00004B/2/P